AQA History

AS
Unit 2

Britain, 1625–1642: the Failure of Absolutism?

David Farr

Series editor
Sally Waller

Thornes

Published in 2008 by:
Nelson Thornes Ltd
Delta Place
27 Bath Road
CHELTENHAM
GL53 7TH
United Kingdom

08 09 10 11 12 / 10 9 8 7 6 5 4 3 2

A catalogue record for this book is available from the British Library

978-0-7487-8285-7

Illustrations by David Russell Illustration, Graham-Cameron Illustration and
Linda Rogers Associates

Page make-up by Thomson Digital

Printed in Croatia by Zrinski

Contents

AQA introduction

Nelson Thornes and AQA

Nelson Thornes has worked in collaboration with AQA to ensure that this book offers you the best support for your AS or A level course and helps you to prepare for your exams. The partnership means that you can be confident that the range of learning, teaching and assessment practice materials has been checked by the senior examining team at AQA before formal approval, and is closely matched to the requirements of your specification.

Blended learning

This book forms a blend with electronic resources: this means that links between topics and activities between the book and the electronic resources help you to work in the way that best suits you, and enable extra support to be provided online. For example, you can test yourself online and feedback from the test will direct you back to the relevant parts of the book.

Electronic resources are available in a simple-to-use online platform called Nelson Thornes learning space. If your school or college has a licence to use the service, you will be given a password through which you can access the materials through any internet connection.

Learning activity

These resources include a variety of interactive and non-interactive activities to support your learning.

Progress tracking

These resources include a variety of tests that you can use to check your knowledge on particular topics (Test yourself) and a range of resources that enable you to analyse and understand examination questions (On your marks…).

Research support

These resources include WebQuests, in which you are assigned a task and provided with a range of web links to use as source material for research.

Study skills

These resources support you to develop a skill that is key for your course, for example planning essays.

When you see an icon, go to Nelson Thornes learning space at www.nelsonthornes.com/aqagce, enter your access details and select your course. The materials are arranged in the same order as the topics in the book, so you can easily find the resources you need.

How to use this book

This book covers the specification for your course and is arranged in a sequence approved by AQA.

The features in this book include:

Timeline

Key events are outlined at the beginning of the book. The events are colour-coded so you can clearly see the categories of change.

Learning objectives

At the beginning of each section you will find a list of learning objectives that contain targets linked to the requirements of the specification.

Key chronology

A short list of dates usually with a focus on a specific event or legislation.

Key profile

The profile of a key person you should be aware of to fully understand the period in question.

Key term

A term that you will need to be able to define and understand.

Did you know?

Interesting information to bring the subject under discussion to life.

Exploring the detail

Information to put further context around the subject under discussion.

A closer look

An in-depth look at a theme, person or event to deepen your understanding. Activities around the extra information may be included.

Sources

Sources to reinforce topics or themes and may provide fact or opinion. They may be quotations from historical works, contemporaries of the period or photographs.

Cross-reference

Links to related content which may offer more detail on the subject in question.

Activity

Various activity types to provide you with different challenges and opportunities to demonstrate both the content and skills you are learning. Some can be worked on individually, some as part of group work and some are designed to specifically "stretch and challenge".

Question

Questions to prompt further discussion on the topic under consideration and are an aid to revision.

Summary questions

Summary questions at the end of each chapter to test your knowledge and allow you to demonstrate your understanding.

AQA Examiner's tip

Hints from AQA examiners to help you with your study and to prepare for your exam.

AQA Examination-style questions

Questions at the end of each section in the style that you can expect in your exam.

Learning outcomes

Learning outcomes at the end of each section remind you what you should know having completed the chapters in that section.

Web links in the book

Because Nelson Thornes is not responsible for third party content online, there may be some changes to this material that are beyond our control. In order for us to ensure that the links referred to in the book are as up-to-date and stable as possible, the web sites provided are usually homepages with supporting instructions on how to reach the relevant pages if necessary.

Please let us know at **webadmin@nelsonthornes.com** if you find a link that doesn't work and we will do our best to correct this at reprint, or to list an alternative site.

Introduction to the History series

When Bruce Bogtrotter in Roald Dahl's *Matilda* was challenged to eat a huge chocolate cake, he just opened his mouth and ploughed in, taking bite after bite and lump after lump until the cake was gone and he was feeling decidedly sick. The picture is not dissimilar to that of some A level history students. They are attracted to history because of its inherent appeal but, when faced with a bulging file and a forthcoming examination, their enjoyment evaporates. They try desperately to cram their brains with an assortment of random facts and subsequently prove unable to control the outpouring of their ill-digested material in the examination.

The books in this series are designed to help students and teachers avoid this feeling of overload and examination panic by breaking down the AQA history specification in such a way that it is easily absorbed. Above all, they are designed to retain and promote students' enthusiasm for history by avoiding a dreary rehash of dates and events. Each book is divided into sections, closely matched to those given in the specification, and the content is further broken down into chapters that present the historical material in a lively and attractive form, offering guidance on the key terms, events and issues, and blending thought-provoking activities and questions in a way designed to advance students' understanding. By encouraging students to think for themselves and to share their ideas with others, as well as helping them to develop the knowledge and skills they will need to pass their examination, this book should ensure that students' learning remains a pleasure rather than an endurance test.

To make the most of what this book provides, students will need to develop efficient study skills from the start and it is worth spending some time considering what these involve:

▨ Good organisation of material in a subject-specific file. Organised notes help develop an organised brain and sensible filing ensures time is not wasted hunting for misplaced material. This book uses cross-references to indicate where material in one chapter has relevance to material in another. Students are advised to adopt the same technique.

▨ A sensible approach to note-making. Students are often too ready to copy large chunks of material from printed books or to download sheaves of printouts from the internet. This series is designed to encourage students to think about the notes they collect and to undertake research with a particular purpose in mind. The activities encourage students

to pick out information that is relevant to the issue being addressed and to avoid making notes on material that is not properly understood.

▨ Taking time to think, which is by far the most important component of study. By encouraging students to think before they write or speak, be it for a written answer, presentation or class debate, students should learn to form opinions and make judgements based on the accumulation of evidence. These are the skills that the examiner will be looking for in the final examination. The beauty of history is that there is rarely a right or wrong answer so, with sufficient evidence, one student's view will count for as much as the next.

▨ Unit 2

Unit 2 promotes the study of significant periods of history in depth. Although the span of years may appear short, the chosen topics are centred on periods of change that raise specific historical issues and they therefore provide an opportunity for students to study in some depth the interrelationships between ideas, individuals, circumstances and other factors that lead to major developments. Appreciating the dynamics of change, and balancing the degree of change against elements of continuity, make for a fascinating and worthwhile study. Students are also required to analyse consequences and draw conclusions about the issues these studies raise. Such themes are, of course, relevant to an understanding of the present and, through such an historical investigation, students will be guided towards a greater appreciation of the world around them today, as well as develop their understanding of the past.

Unit 2 is tested by a 1 hour 30 minute paper containing three questions. The first question is compulsory and based on sources, while the remaining two, of which students will need to choose one, are two-part questions as described in Table 1. Plentiful sources are included throughout this book to give students some familiarity with contemporary and historiographical material, and activities and suggestions are provided to enable students to develop the required examination skills. Students should familiarise themselves with the question breakdown, additional hints and marking criteria given below before attempting any of the practice examination-style questions at the end of each section.

Answers will be marked according to a scheme based on 'levels of response'. This means that the answer will be assessed according to which level best matches the historical skills displayed, taking both knowledge and understanding into account. All students should have a copy of these criteria and need to use them wisely.

Table 1 *Unit 2: style of questions and marks available*

Unit 2	Question	Marks	Question type	Question stem	Hints for students
Question 1 based on three sources of c.300–350 words in total	(a)	12	This question involves the comparison of two sources	Explain how far the views in Source B differ from those in Source A in relation to…	Take pains to avoid simply writing out what each source says with limited direct comment. Instead, you should try to find two or three points of comparison and illustrate these with reference to the sources. You should also look for any underlying similarities. In your conclusion, you will need to make it clear exactly 'how far' the views differ
Question 1	(b)	24	This requires use of the sources and own knowledge and asks for an explanation that shows awareness that issues and events can provoke differing views and explanations	How far… How important was… How successful…	This answer needs to be planned as you will need to develop an argument in your answer and show balanced judgement. Try to set out your argument in the introduction and, as you develop your ideas through your paragraphs, support your opinions with detailed evidence. Your conclusion should flow naturally and provide supported judgement. The sources should be used as 'evidence' throughout your answer. Do ensure you refer to them all
Question 2 and 3	(a)	12	This question is focused on a narrow issue within the period studied and requires an explanation	Explain why…	Make sure you explain 'why', not 'how', and try to order your answer in a way that shows you understand the inter-linkage of factors and which are the most important. You should try to reach an overall judgement/ conclusion
Question 2 and 3	(b)	24	This question is broader and asks for analysis and explanation with appropriate judgement. The question requires an awareness of debate over issues	A quotation in the form of a judgement on a key development or issue will be given and candidates asked: Explain why you agree or disagree with this view	This answer needs to be planned as you will need to show balanced judgement. Try to think of points that agree and disagree and decide which way you will argue. Set out your argument in the introduction and support it through your paragraphs, giving the alternative picture too but showing why your view is the more convincing. Your conclusion should flow naturally from what you have written

Marking criteria

Question 1(a)

Level 1 Answers either briefly paraphrase/describe the content of the two sources or identify simple comparison(s) between the sources. Skills of written communication will be weak. *(0–2 marks)*

Level 2 Responses will compare the views expressed in the two sources and identify some differences and/or similarities. There may be some limited own knowledge. Answers will be coherent but weakly expressed. *(3–6 marks)*

Level 3 Responses will compare the views expressed in the two sources, identifying differences **and** similarities and using own knowledge to explain and evaluate these. Answers will, for the most part, be clearly expressed. *(7–9 marks)*

Level 4 Responses will make a developed comparison between the views expressed in the two sources **and** own knowledge will apply to evaluate and to demonstrate a good contextual understanding. Answers will, for the most part, show good skills of written communication. *(10–12 marks)*

Question 1(b)

Level 1 Answers may be based on sources or on own knowledge alone, or they may comprise an undeveloped mixture of the two. They may contain some descriptive material which is only loosely linked to the focus of the question or they may address only a part of the question. Alternatively, there may be some explicit comment with little, if any, appropriate support. Answers are likely to be generalised and assertive. There will be little, if any, awareness of differing historical interpretations. The response will be limited in development and skills of written communication will be weak. *(0–6 marks)*

Level 2 Answers may be based on sources or on own knowledge alone, or they may contain a mixture of the two. They may be almost entirely descriptive with few explicit links to the focus of the question. Alternatively, they may contain some explicit comment with relevant but limited support. They will display limited understanding of differing historical interpretations. Answers will be coherent but weakly expressed and/or poorly structured. *(7–11 marks)*

Level 3 Answers will show a developed understanding of the demands of the question using evidence from **both** the sources **and** own knowledge. They will provide some assessment backed by relevant and appropriately selected evidence, but they will lack depth and/or balance. There will be some understanding of varying historical interpretations. Answers will, for the most part, be clearly expressed and show some organisation in the presentation of material. *(12–16 marks)*

Level 4 Answers will show explicit understanding of the demands of the question. They will develop a balanced argument backed by a good range of appropriately selected evidence from the sources and own knowledge, and a good understanding of historical interpretations. Answers will, for the most part, show organisation and good skills of written communication. *(17–21 marks)*

Level 5 Answers will be well focused and closely argued. The arguments will be supported by precisely selected evidence from the sources and own knowledge, incorporating well-developed understanding of historical interpretations and debate. Answers will, for the most part, be carefully organised and fluently written, using appropriate vocabulary. *(22–24 marks)*

Question 2(a) and 3(a)

Level 1 Answers will contain either some descriptive material which is only loosely linked to the focus of the question or some explicit comment with little, if any, appropriate support. Answers are likely to be generalised and assertive. The response will be limited in development and skills of written communication will be weak. *(0–2 marks)*

Level 2 Answers will demonstrate some knowledge and understanding of the demands of the question. They will either be almost entirely descriptive with few explicit links to the question **or** they provide some explanations backed by evidence that is limited in range and/or depth. Answers will be coherent but weakly expressed and/or poorly structured. *(3–6 marks)*

Level 3 Answers will demonstrate good understanding of the demands of the question providing relevant explanations backed by appropriately selected information, although this may not be full or comprehensive. Answers will, for the most part, be clearly expressed and show some organisation in the presentation of material. *(7–9 marks)*

Level 4 Answers will be well focused, identifying a range of specific explanations backed by precise evidence and demonstrating good understanding of the connections and links between events/issues. Answers will, for the most part, be well written and organised. *(10–12 marks)*

Question 2(b) and 3(b)

Level 1 Answers may **either** contain some descriptive material which is only loosely linked to the focus of the question **or** they may address only a limited part of the period of the question. Alternatively, there may be some explicit comment with little, if any, appropriate support. Answers are likely to be generalised and assertive. There will be little, if any, awareness of different historical interpretations. The response will be limited in development and skills of written communication will be weak. *(0–6 marks)*

Level 2 Answers will show some understanding of the demands of the question. They will either be almost entirely descriptive with few explicit links to the question **or** they contain some explicit comment with relevant but limited support. They will display limited understanding of differing historical interpretations. Answers will be coherent but weakly expressed and/or poorly structured.   *(7–11 marks)*

Level 3 Answers will show a developed understanding of the demands of the question. They will provide some assessment, backed by relevant and appropriately selected evidence, but they will lack depth and/or balance. There will be some understanding of varying historical interpretations. Answers will, for the most part, be clearly expressed and show some organisation in the presentation of material.   *(12–16 marks)*

Level 4 Answers will show explicit understanding of the demands of the question. They will develop a balanced argument backed by a good range of appropriately selected evidence and a good understanding of historical interpretations. Answers will, for the most part, show organisation and good skills of written communication.   *(17–21 marks)*

Level 5 Answers will be well focused and closely argued. The arguments will be supported by precisely selected evidence leading to a relevant conclusion/judgement, incorporating well-developed understanding of historical interpretations and debate. Answers will, for the most part, be carefully organised and fluently written, using appropriate vocabulary.   *(22–24 marks)*

Introduction to this book

Fig. 1 *James I of England and James VI of Scotland*

The outbreak of the Thirty Years' War

In 1618, religious war between Catholics and Protestants engulfed Europe. Since the **Reformation** and the emergence of Protestantism, religion had divided the European States against each other and internally. The most disputed area, 'Germany', consisted of 329 separate States. Although the conflict was centred here, many European States were drawn in by their religious stance or alliances (Table 1).

Table 1 *Major European States and their divisions during the Thirty Years' War, 1618–48*

Country	State religion	Aligned with during war
Spain	Catholic	Catholic/Habsburgs
France	Catholic	Protestant/anti-Habsburg from 1635
Sweden	Protestant	Protestant/anti-Habsburg
Dutch Republic	Protestant	Protestant/anti-Habsburg
North German States	Mainly Protestant	Protestant/anti-Habsburg
South German States	Mainly Catholic	Catholic/Habsburgs
Denmark	Protestant	Protestant/anti-Habsburg

The main European political rivalry between Spain and France cut across religious lines. The Habsburgs who ruled Spain also controlled what are now known as Austria, Belgium (then known as the Spanish Netherlands), as well as parts of Italy. With their South American empire, Spain was a world power. Through their influence, Spain had ensured that the Holy Roman Emperor, the official leader of all German States, was also a Habsburg. In 1618, Emperor Rudolph died and was replaced by a more rigid Catholic, Ferdinand.

The European conflict was an issue for King James I of England because his daughter, Elizabeth, was married to a Protestant German prince, Frederick of **the Palatinate**.

Key profile

James Stuart

James Stuart became King James VI of Scotland in 1566. In 1603, when the last Tudor, Elizabeth I, died childless, James also succeeded to the English throne as King James I, having a claim through his great-grandmother, Margaret Tudor, sister of Henry VIII, who had married the Scottish King James IV. A successful ruler, James was pragmatic enough to realise that he needed to work with parliament.

Frederick had, in part, caused the war by accepting the crown of Bohemia when it was offered to him by those who had rebelled against the Catholic Holy Roman Emperor Ferdinand Habsburg, whose title traditionally meant that his election as King of Bohemia should have been a formality. The Holy Roman Emperor was, naturally enough, the leader of the Holy Roman Empire. The Empire covered a large area of central Europe from the Baltic to the Alps and from France to Poland. This Empire was covered by a mix of princedoms and States, some of whom in theory elected the Emperor but in reality, by the 17th century, the title was controlled by the Habsburg family.

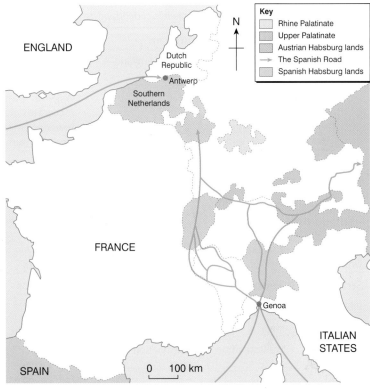

Fig. 2 *The Palatinate in Europe*

After a major Catholic victory at the Battle of White Mountain in October 1620, Frederick and Elizabeth were forced into exile while the Palatinate was occupied by the Spanish and Ferdinand's Imperial army. The Palatinate was of key strategic significance being central to the 'Spanish Road', Spain's route to attack the Dutch Republic. James thus had not only religious reasons, as a Protestant king, but also dynastic (family) reasons, to intervene in the crisis. Despite pressure from parliament to join the war against the Catholics, James resisted.

In domestic politics the European crisis raised the inter-related themes of religion, foreign policy, finance and favourites, which were to be central to the politics of the years 1621–9.

■ Religion, foreign policy, finance and favourites

Religion

Religion was a key issue in the 17th century. From Henry VIII's Reformation, England became a predominantly Protestant country. Alongside a significant minority of remaining Catholics, there were, however, differences between Protestants.

James I maintained a balanced broad Church so that the majority of Protestants felt they could belong to the State Church and would not have to oppose the King as Supreme Governor, ruler, of the Church. The anti-Calvinists, more regularly known as Arminians, or under Charles as the Laudians, were those Protestant conservatives who did not wish the Reformation to go any further, indeed they wanted elements of the pre-Reformation Church brought back. They put ceremonies above sermons and criticised the key Calvinist doctrine of predestination, i.e. that people's fate after death had already been decided by God no matter what good they might do. Unlike the majority of English Protestants, they did not regard the Catholic Church as evil but as the 'mother church' that had gone off track. Charles allowed them to dominate the Church. This broke the 'Jacobethan balance' (the moderate Calvinist broad Church constructed by Elizabeth I and maintained by James I). Even moderate Anglicans/Calvinists now felt alienated.

■ Exploring the detail

Calvinism

Named after John Calvin (1509–64), the most influential Protestant reformer apart from Martin Luther, who established Geneva as a centre of Protestantism. Central to Calvinism was predestination and the discipline imposed on members of the Church by the elders who ran the Church. Calvinism became the branch of Protestantism predominant in the Church of England.

Table 2 *Main religious groupings of England, Scotland and Ireland*

Key features	Protestant	Protestant	Protestant	Protestant	Catholic
	Scotland	Church of England	Church of England	Church of England	
	Presbyterian	Puritan	'Anglican' with a moderate Calvinist-based theology but an Episcopal structure (bishops)	Anti-Calvinists or Arminians	Catholic
Head	No head	Monarch	Monarch	Monarch	Pope
Governors	Elders	Bishops, but many Puritans were wary of them and saw the minister as the key figure	Bishops	Bishops	Cardinals; bishops
Dress	Plain	Plain	Vestments	Vestments	Vestments
Service	Sermon	Sermon	Communion	Communion	Latin Mass
Bible	English	English	English	English	Latin
Building	Plain	Plain	Decoration	Decoration	Decoration
Salvation	Predestination	Predestination	A range of approaches – through Faith, good works, open to all, predestination	Open to all to accept	Through Faith, good works
Numbers In England	Minority; main religion of Scotland	An important minority in England. Within those classed as 'Puritan' there were also different approaches	Majority. As the religion of the majority, there were different approaches to all the features listed	Minority, but gained influence under Charles	Minority. Majority in Ireland, small minorities in England and Scotland

Fig. 3 *Foxe's Book of Martyrs*

All English Protestants shared a general anti-Catholicism that was a result of the Reformation, a reaction to the burning of Protestants when England had briefly been returned to Catholicism by 'Bloody' Mary I (1553–8) and war against Catholic Spain during Elizabeth's reign. This anti-Catholicism was the context from which the majority of the English population reacted to religious war in Europe.

The more radical Protestants, the Puritans, were the most virulent in their anti-Catholicism. For them, the Pope, the head of the Catholic Church, was the anti-Christ.

For most Protestants, the anti-Calvinist Arminians were seen as closet Catholics. Charles' siding with them was thus politically dangerous when set in context of his 1625 marriage to the Catholic French princess Henrietta Maria and his foreign policy in the years 1625 to 1629.

Key profile

Henrietta Maria

Daughter of Henry IV of France, Henrietta Maria (1606–69) married Charles in 1625. The marriage was part of James I's foreign policy. Having failed to secure a marriage between Charles and a Spanish princess, which he believed would help him negotiate peace for Europe, a marriage was secured with the French, the main rivals of Spain. This was to signal a more aggressive stance to Spain as part of the attempt to recover the Palatinate. After some initial tension, partly as a result of Charles' reliance on Buckingham, Henrietta Maria and Charles became very close. This, however, had some negative political impact as Henrietta Maria was regarded as influencing Charles towards Catholicism and absolutism. Her advice to Charles during the crisis of 1637 to 1642 was invariably to take a hard line.

Foreign policy

The crucial issue since 1618 had been the Thirty Years' War. James I, recognising the political and financial dangers of involvement, had avoided it, despite parliamentary pressure. In the 1624 parliament, Prince Charles and the Duke of Buckingham, the most powerful man in England beside the King, had sided with MPs who wanted war. When Charles came to the throne, he took the country to war, first against Spain, then against France and Spain. This was to have serious political consequences. For example, to finance these, Charles turned to **prerogative** income.

Finance

A century of inflation, price rises, meant that English monarchs increasingly found their income could not meet their expenses, especially foreign policy. Substantial funds could only be raised through parliamentary subsidy. Parliament, however, was normally reluctant to vote subsidies as they would have to raise the money through taxing the 'political nation'. This essentially encompassed those who had political influence through their wealth. Only merchants, lawyers, but especially the gentry, landowners of varying degrees, and those above them, the aristocracy, were represented in and by parliament. Although in theory MPs represented all those in the area for which they had been selected, in reality they were only concerned with the interests of the ruling elite. Only the wealthy had to pay a parliamentary subsidy, which also meant that it was not in their interests to grant subsidies to the monarch. The limits of parliamentary subsidies forced monarchs to exploit their prerogative income, money raised on their rights as monarchs.

Did you know?

The Pope as the anti-Christ

James I did much to establish the Pope as the anti-Christ in two of his works, *A Paraphrase Upon the Revelation of the Apostle Saint John* and *A Premonition to all most Mighty Monarchies.*

Key term

Prerogative: the monarch's powers not dependent on parliament. They included the right to choose ministers, call and dissolve parliament, decide foreign policy and raise money in various ways.

Table 3 *The main forms of crown income*

Income	Definition
Crown lands	The crown had sold much land or rented it out on long leases at a fixed rent, thus reducing the income and preventing the updating of the rents in line with inflation
Customs duties	Tax income from goods imported into the country. The crown had sold the right to collect them (customs farming) for short-term payment.
Feudal dues	Ancient rights like wardship, where the crown had the right to control an estate that was inherited by an heir under 21 years
Parliamentary subsidy	Money voted by parliament for emergencies like war

Prerogative income raised parliamentarian concerns that if the monarch became self-sufficient, they could establish themselves as **absolute**, i.e. in no need of a parliament.

■ Favourites

Charles' relationship with key individuals also had an important role in shaping the politics of his reign. Initially, Charles was close to Buckingham, his father's **favourite**.

■ Key profile

George Villiers, Duke of Buckingham

Buckingham (1592–1628) came to prominence in 1616 because James I liked him. From 1620, he became closer to James' son, Prince Charles. In 1623, they travelled together to Madrid in an attempt to secure a marriage between Charles and the Spanish princess, Maria. This experience seems to have bound them closer and, when James died in 1625, Buckingham became the favourite of the new King, Charles I. As Lord High Admiral, Buckingham showed himself to be an effective administrator but was seen as responsible for foreign policy failures. Attacked by parliament he was defended by Charles but in 1628 Buckingham was assassinated by a disgruntled soldier.

The basis of the relationship between Buckingham and Charles was less overtly sexual than the one the favourite had had with James I. From 1620, James took a role in reconciling his favourite and Charles who, until that point had a difficult relationship. Indeed, it was in Buckingham's interest to develop his links with the heir to the throne. Buckingham was allowed a predominant role in the management of royal patronage, which forced others to look to parliament as a forum to pursue their interests. Buckingham's pre-eminence also led to court **faction**, disrupting the parliaments of 1621–9.

■ The 1621 parliament

At the start of King James' 1621 parliament, MPs focused on the abuse of monopolies, partly as a means of attacking Buckingham. Monopolies referred to the way a monarch could grant the sole right to import or produce a good to an individual or group. Monopolies were an issue in the 1621 parliament because England was in trade depression and they had been particularly exploited by many courtiers. As part of factional infighting, courtiers made monopolies a parliamentary issue as a means of attacking each other. Buckingham, with Edward Coke and Lionel Cranfield, encouraged parliament to impeach their rival Francis Bacon over monopolies. Monopolies are, therefore, an indication that the politics of this period were not necessarily a crown–parliament split, but more regularly factional political infighting.

Foreign policy was part of the monarch's prerogative and therefore parliament had no right to discuss it. Foreign policy became a parliamentary issue, however, when James implied that MPs could discuss it. He did this to try to frighten the Spanish into agreeing to a 'Spanish match', a dynastic marriage between Prince Charles and a Spanish princess. James saw this as a means to negotiate between Protestants and Catholics to end the European conflict. The Commons, however, went further than James had anticipated and produced a Petition on 3 December 1621 criticising the Spanish match. In response, James stated that foreign policy was part of his prerogative and not for discussion. This provoked a Commons' Protestation on 18 December 1621 declaring their 'undoubted birthright' to discuss such matters. Foreign policy had become a source of constitutional conflict between the crown's prerogative and parliament's privileges, i.e. their rights. Angered by parliament's Protestation, James used his prerogative to rip the document from the Commons' Journal, their book of record, and dissolved parliament.

The 1624 parliament

In 1624, Charles and Buckingham were deeply involved in the main subject of debate, foreign policy. The crucial issue remained whether England should intervene in the European war. Following their visit to Madrid in 1623, by which they hoped to secure the Spanish match but had failed, both Charles and Buckingham converted to an anti-Spanish policy.

In 1624, their alignment with the majority of MPs who wanted war made Charles, on the surface, politically popular. James warned his son and favourite that their alliance with MPs could be politically damaging in the long term because of the complications of the inter-related issues of foreign policy, religion and finance. These issues were, indeed, to bedevil the first four years of Charles' reign as his personality exacerbated the tensions raised by the question of whether to intervene in the European conflict.

> In 1625 Charles I inherited three kingdoms divided in religion and in which royal income remained barely adequate to cover peacetime expenses. However, he also inherited three kingdoms which had enjoyed a generation of peace.

1   *Gaunt, P., **The British Civil Wars, 1637–1651**, 1997*

> Charles' inheritance was by no means an impossible one, but Charles' throne was particularly vulnerable because he ruled over three disparate kingdoms, and because in England successful government depended on consent. The task before him called for insight, judgement, tact, flair, and dedication. He possessed the last quality in abundance, but he was short of all the others.

2   *Woolrych, A., **Britain in Revolution**, 2002*

A lot would depend on what kind of man, and therefore king, Charles I was.

Timeline

Black – politics; red – finance; Blue – religion; Green – foreign policy. In the seventeenth century all these factors were very much interlinked, religion was, for example, politics.

1618	1621	1623	1624	1625	1625	1625	1625
Outbreak of the Thirty Years' War in Europe	James I's third parliament – Commons' petition and protestation as tension between crown and parliament rises over foreign policy	The Madrid trip. Charles and Buckingham go to Madrid to secure the 'Spanish match', a proposed marriage of Prince Charles and the Spanish Princess Maria	James I's fourth parliament – continued pressure on James to intervene in the European war	Death of James I	Charles' marriage to Henrietta Maria	First parliament – tonnage and poundage voted for one year only	Montagu attacked in parliament, appointed royal chaplain by Charles

1628	1628	1628	1628	1628	1629	1629	1629
Third parliament	Petition of Right	Laud made Bishop of London	Buckingham assassinated	Wentworth made President of the Council of the North	Second session of third parliament	Three Resolutions	Treaty of Susa – peace with France

1633	1633	1634	1634	1634	1634	1635	1635	1636	1636
Re-issue of *Book of Sports*	St Gregory's case	Forest fines	Ship money on coastal towns and counties	Irish convocation adopts Thirty-nine Articles	Lord Balmerino punished	New *Book of Rates* issued	Ship money extended inland	Scottish canons promulgated	Bishop Juxon appointed Lord Treasurer

1640	1640	1640	1640	1641	1641	1641	1641
13 April to 5 May Short parliament	**August** Cumbernauld Band; Second Bishops' War – Treaty of Ripon	**November** Long parliament; Strafford impeached	**December** London Root and Branch Petition; Laud impeached	**February** Triennial Act	**May** Protestation Oath; Army plot; death of Bedford	**10 May** Act of Attainder	**June** Ten Propositions

1642	1642	1642	1642	1642
March Militia ordinance	**April** Hull	**June** Nineteen Propositions; commissions of array	**18 June** Answer to the Nineteen Propositions	**August** Nottingham: Charles raises his standard and civil war begins

1625	1625	1626	1626	1626	1627	1627	1627
Attacks on Buckingham in parliament	Unsuccessful attack on Spanish port Cadiz	Second parliament – attempted impeachment of Buckingham	York House Conference to discuss religion	Forced loan	Declaration of war against France	Attempt to help the Huguenots of La Rochelle	Five Knights' Case

1630	1630	1631	1632	1633	1633	1633
Distraint of knighthood fines	Treaty of Madrid – peace with Spain	*Book of Orders*	Wentworth made Lord Deputy of Ireland	Prynne's Histrio-mastix	Charles crowned in Scotland	Laud made Archbishop of Canterbury

1637	1637	1637	1638	1638	1639	1639	1639
Trial of Prynne, Bastwick and Burton	Bishop Williams fined for attacking Laud's altar policy	**July** Introduction of the *New Prayer Book* in Edinburgh	National Covenant drawn up	Hampden's case	First Bishops' War – pacification of Berwick	Growing resistance to ship money	Wentworth arrives in England – created Earl of Strafford (1640)

1641	1641	1641	1641	1641	1642	1642	1642
Abolition of Star Chamber; ship money made illegal	**August** Charles leaves for Scotland – the 'Incident'	**October/ November** Irish Rebellion; Second army plot	**22–3 November** Grand Remonstrance, passed with votes 159–148	Charles returns to London	**2 January** Charles offers Pym chancellorship	**4 January** Five Members' Coup	**February** Henrietta Maria leaves England

1 Parliaments and policy, 1625–6

Fig. 1 *Charles I's coronation procession, 1625*

In the 1624 parliament, Prince Charles was, on the surface, in tune with calls of MPs for intervention in the Thirty Years' War. Within a year of his becoming king, however, there was tension between Charles and his first parliament over religion, finance and foreign policy. In 1625, the English attack on the Spanish port of Cadiz descended into chaos when more English troops died from local Spanish wine than Spanish gunfire.

The new King, Charles I

Historians stress that Charles was a very different man and king to his politically astute father. Sharpe has commented that he 'was in many respects a complete contrast to his father' and Cogswell has referred to Charles being James' 'mirror opposite'. Young has gone as far to argue that 'it was not just that Charles happened to be the opposite of his father; he consciously set out to make himself the opposite'. Charles' differences were rooted in his personality. In a time of personal monarchy, when the monarch was the centre of power and thus initiated policy, this had a real political effect.

In contrast with his gregarious father, Charles was shy and hampered by a speech defect. Both led to him being unapproachable and, more damaging, uncommunicative with parliament. Here, his intentions and actions often went unexplained, leaving others to interpret them.

Fig. 2 *Charles' weaknesses*

Key chronology

1625 First parliament – tonnage and poundage voted for one year only.

Unsuccessful expedition to Cadiz.

1626 Second parliament – attempted impeachment of Buckingham.

York House Conference.

Forced loan.

1627 Declaration of war against France. La Rochelle.

Five Knights' Case.

1628 Third parliament – Petition of Right.

Laud made Bishop of London.

Buckingham assassinated.

1629 Second session of third parliament.

Three Resolutions.

Charles had an inferiority complex that made him overstress his prerogative. Charles, because of his insecurity, had none of James' political shrewdness or flexibility. He did not know the meaning of compromise. Charles seemed unable to understand viewpoints that differed from his own and thought more in a conspiracy theory mentality that interpreted the slightest hint of criticism as sedition.

The political consequences of Charles' character were clear in the first years of his reign. The period 1625–9 witnessed a breakdown in the relationship between crown and parliament.

Where James was an informal, approachable man, Charles was cold, withdrawn, and shifty. He was a weakling brought up in the shadow of an accomplished elder brother who died of smallpox when Charles was 12. Charles was short, a stammerer, a man of deep indecision who tried to simplify the world around him by persuading himself that where the king led by example and where order and uniformity were set forth, obedience and peace would follow. He was one of those politicians so confident of his own motives and actions, that he saw no need to explain his actions or justify his conduct to his people.

1 Morrill, J., *Stuart Britain. A Very Short Introduction, 2000*

Charles was a cold, formal figure who rarely sought to explain himself or to win affection. Instead, he emphasised the majesty of the crown and required unquestioning obedience. He often failed to understand viewpoints different from his own and instead equated them with disloyalty. Possessing none of his father's willingness to compromise and conciliate, he proceeded even when a policy was arousing great opposition or was proving unworkable.

2 Gaunt, P., *The British Civil Wars, 1637–51, 1997*

The parliaments of 1625 and 1626: finance, foreign policy, favourites and Arminianism

In 1624, Prince Charles appeared to have a good working relationship with parliament. In the first four years of his reign, however, this relationship broke down. The reasons for the breakdown of the relationship between crown and parliament lay in the themes that had bedevilled the later years of James I: finance; foreign policy; favourites; and Arminianism. What had been added to this volatile mix, however, was a very different king – Charles I.

When Charles I came to the throne the key issue he faced, like his father, was foreign policy. Unlike his father, however, Charles planned to go to war with Spain. Charles' anti-Spanish policy had four parts:

Activity

Source analysis

1 Explain how far the views in Source 2 differ from those in Source 1 in relation to Charles' personality.

2 What possible political consequences for Charles' relationship with parliament are suggested in both sources that derive from Charles' personality?

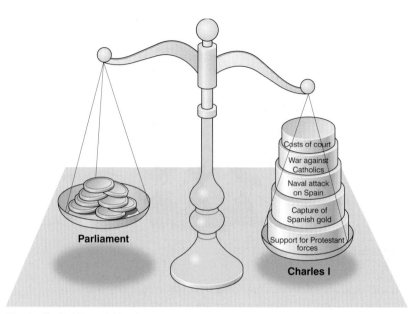

Fig. 3 *Charles' financial burden*

1 Financial backing for his uncle Christian IV of Denmark to attack the Catholics through northern Germany.
2 Financial support for the Protestant Dutch.
3 Construction of a force of about 6,000 Englishmen to be led by a German mercenary, Count Mansfeld.
4 A naval attack on Spain aimed at capturing their transport of gold from South America.

The 1625 parliament

Charles planned war expenditure of £1m. For this, he needed the cooperation of his first parliament but he refused to explain his position or ask for a specific subsidy. The Commons' distrust was shown by the grant of only two subsidies, about £140,000, and tonnage and poundage, a customs tax, for one year only instead of the usual grant for the life of the new monarch. For parliament, this limited grant was a way to give them time to discuss reform of customs duties and other matters that concerned them. The limited grant was also directed at Buckingham more than Charles. Tonnage and poundage as a form of customs duty normally contributed to naval protection and Buckingham, as Lord High Admiral, appeared to be failing in his responsibility. Charles, however, regarded the limited grant of tonnage and poundage as a direct attack on his prerogative. He felt that parliament was being too influenced by men whom he regarded as radicals, like Sir Robert Phelips and Sir Edward Coke, who were particularly responsible for persuading the Commons to only vote tonnage and poundage for one year. Charles decided to ignore parliament and continue to collect tonnage and poundage after the first year.

Apart from finance, the other issues for parliament were Buckingham and religion. Buckingham was a source of tension because of the enormous influence he had wielded since he first emerged as James I's favourite in 1616. Later, there were rumours that Buckingham had bewitched the King.

Buckingham's power had been extended in the early 1620s and continued under Charles I.

Fig. 4 *George Villiers, Ist Duke of Buckingham (1592–1628)*

■ **Did you know?**
Witchcraft

There remained a widespread belief in witchcraft in the period. James I as King of Scotland had written a book, *Demonolgie* (1597), on witchcraft. It has been estimated that there were between 40,000 to 50,000 executions across Europe for witchcraft.

Buckingham may feel assured that the favour of the new King will be extended to him. This is already shown by the most transparent evidence. He is with his Majesty all day; he sleeps in a room adjoining to the royal chamber; he has been confirmed in all his offices which are numerous and of the highest importance; and he has also been made Gentleman of the **Bedchamber**, and has received the golden key, the emblem of his office, so that he can, whenever he pleases, and at any hour, enter that chamber as well as any other part of the palace occupied by his Majesty. In short, nothing is done without him.

> **3**　　'Report of the Tuscan Ambassador, 1625' in Quintrell, B., **Charles I 1625–1640**, 1993

Key term

Bedchamber: the monarch's most private chamber and thereby the most private part of the court. Access to this part of the court was therefore most sought after in a system where political influence was reliant on access to the monarch. Courtiers competed to serve the monarch as part of the Bedchamber. Favourites such as Buckingham had been able to secure most access to the monarch.

Parliament also attacked Charles' support of the Arminian cleric Richard Montagu. Montagu's book of 1624, *An Old Gagg for a New Goose*, had put forward the anti-Calvinist argument, much to the disgust of Puritans but also other Protestants, that there were many similarities between Catholicism and the Church of England. Montagu repeated his argument in a new work of 1625, *Appello Caesarem*. In response to parliamentary attacks on Montagu, Charles provocatively appointed him as his royal chaplain. This was a clear statement of Charles' approval of anti-Calvinism. Charles appeared unaware of the problems that could arise over religion.

Charles created many of the problems with the 1625 parliament. Charles would not make any concessions, he did not consult the court's most influential supporters in the countryside, and he did not engage with leading figures in the Commons like Dudley Digges and Edward Sandys. Charles' response to parliamentary criticism of Buckingham and Montagu was to dissolve (i.e. end the sitting of) parliament.

Activity

Source analysis

1 What does Source 3 suggest about the influence of Buckingham in the years 1625 to 1628?

2 How useful is this source as evidence of Buckingham's influence?

The York House Conference, 1626

At the request of the puritan nobleman the Earl of Warwick, and to avoid further pressure in parliament on religious issues, Buckingham chaired a theological debate at his London home, York House, in February 1626. The focus was on the writings of Montagu. For Warwick, the Conference was designed to persuade Charles away from the anti-Calvinism of Arminians like Montagu. Buckingham, however, although he had links to Warwick, took a stance in support of the leading anti-Calvinist, William Laud. He did this to reinforce his political relationship with Charles. As favourite, his power was really dependent on the favour of the King. From the Conference, it was clear that Charles I, who did not even consider that he should attend a discussion on his religious policy, would not be dissuaded from supporting the anti-Calvinist Arminians.

The full impact of the 'Arminian revolution' was not felt until the 1630s. But the die was cast with the displacement of Calvinism as the doctrinal orthodoxy in the opening months of the reign. Charles' role in this was critical and it demonstrated one of the most striking features of his style of kingship – his refusal to compromise where he believed his conscience was engaged or his God given royal authority was at stake.

> **4**　　Cust, R., **Charles I**, 2005

Fig. 5 *A Puritan family. Father teaching his family to sing psalms rather than 'vayne and tryflying ballades'*

■ Did you know?

Astrology in the 17th century

Astrology was popular in the period. In a sermon to the 1628 parliament, William Laud referred to the conjunction of Saturn and Mars. In the diary he kept, he noted astrological data. Buckingham had his own astrologer, Dr John Lambe, who, in June 1628, was beaten through the streets of London because of his association with the favourite. He died as a result of his injuries.

■ Cross-reference

For the **foreign policy disaster** at La Rochelle, see page 21.

For profiles of **Coke** and **Wentworth** see pages 24 and 64. Also see chart of the structure of local government on page 39.

■ Foreign policy failure: Cadiz

Charles' problems with the 1625 parliament were followed by disaster in his foreign policy.

- The troops for the German mercenary, Mansfeld, were raised by force and shipped to Holland with no training and limited equipment. 4,000 out of 6,000 troops died of disease and starvation.

- In August 1626, the Danish forces of Christian IV were defeated by Catholic forces.

- The English fleet sailed under the command of Edward Cecil in September, but failed to take the Spanish port of Cadiz or capture the Spanish treasure fleet. More English troops were actually lost at Cadiz to local Spanish wine and lack of food than enemy gunfire.

- The failure to capture the Spanish fleet transporting gold from its South American colonies was a particular blow for Charles as it made it much more necessary to call another parliament for finance. The foreign policy failure at Cadiz was the backdrop for the 1626 parliament. Charles was to experience another major foreign policy failure within a year of the Cadiz fiasco, this time at La Rochelle off the coast of France.

The 1626 parliament

Some of Charles' parliamentary critics of 1625, notably Sir Edward Coke and Thomas Wentworth, had been removed by ensuring they

Fig. 6 *London Bridge, 1630*

Key term

Recusants: those who refused to attend the compulsory Sunday Church of England service, particularly Catholics. The initial punishment for recusants was usually a fine that provided the crown with more income. Recusants could also be imprisoned.

were picked as Sheriffs. Sheriffs were responsible for organising the polls and therefore could not stand for election. Buckingham had also tried to reinforce his position by using his influence to remove anyone he regarded as a potential threat. At court, figures like Lord Keeper John Williams and the Earl of Arundel, who were not supporters of Buckingham, were respectively dismissed and arrested. The extent of Buckingham's influence was also illustrated by his ability to purge those in local government, lord lieutenants and deputy lord lieutenants, whom he regarded as opponents.

Charles immediately antagonised the 1626 parliament by getting the anti-Calvinist William Laud to preach the opening sermon. In his sermon, Laud stressed obedience to the King.

Charles did also try to appease his parliamentary critics by ordering the punishment of **recusants** and threatening the return of English ships used against the Protestant French Huguenots of La Rochelle, thereby sparking a possible war against the French.

While parliament sought to place the blame for foreign policy failure on Buckingham as Lord High Admiral, Charles regarded parliament as partly to blame for the failure due to their lack of funding.

Exploring the detail

The Huguenots

The Huguenots were French Protestants who were a persecuted minority in their own country because the French King, Louis XIII, and the majority of the population were Catholics. Seeing them as a threat, it eventually became the policy of the French crown to wipe out the Huguenots. The main base of the Huguenots was the coastal town stronghold on the west of France, La Rochelle.

> This war which grows full of danger was not entered upon rashly and without advice, but by the counsel of both Houses of Parliament. Upon their persuasions and promises of all assistance and supply we readily undertook and effected and cannot now be left in that business but with sin and shame of all men.

5   *Charles I addressing George Abbot, Archbishop of Canterbury in September 1626. From Quintrell, B.,* **Charles I 1625–1640***, 1993*

In some ways, Charles was right to feel bitter about parliament's financing of his foreign policy. Their reluctance to grant subsidies was perhaps a sign that their calls for war were little more than rhetoric. MPs were reluctant to vote the huge sums needed for the kind of war that might really recover the Palatinate and preferred to think in terms of limited, and therefore cheaper, naval engagements. Large subsidies would be paid by the gentry and therefore MPs had a vested financial interest in not funding the kind of war that was needed. What made Charles even more antagonistic to the 1626 parliament was, however, that despite his attempts at compromise by indicating a shift to an anti-French policy, MPs launched impeachment proceedings against Buckingham.

Impeachment was a medieval parliamentary procedure that had been revived in the 1621 and 1624 parliaments by Buckingham himself to

Fig. 7 *George Abbot (1562–1633) was an English divine and Archbishop of Canterbury*

Did you know?

In 1605, George Abbot, the future Archbishop of Canterbury, wrote a geography textbook.

remove two of his rivals at court. It was a method whereby a crown minister could be tried by the House of Lords on charges outlined in a petition from the Commons. The advantage of this process was that it removed the trial from the ordinary courts that were all under the crown's prerogative.

> His Majesty cannot believe that the aim is at the Duke of Buckingham, but findeth that these proceedings do directly wound the honour and judgment of himself and his father.

  Charles' thoughts relating to parliament, 1626. Taken from
Scarboro, D., **England 1625–1660**, 2005

■ Activity

Talking point

Why did Charles state that parliament's attack on Buckingham was also an attack on himself and his father, James I?

Sir John Eliot particularly directed the attack on Buckingham in the Commons. In the Lords there was support for the Earl of Arundel, whom Buckingham had had arrested. One Dr Turner MP, a client of Arundel, produced six articles that directly attacked Buckingham's influence. More threatening to Buckingham and Charles was, however, the Earl of Bristol. Bristol had been the ambassador to Spain when Charles and Buckingham had arrived in Madrid in 1623 to try to secure the Spanish match. Bristol therefore knew that, while in Madrid, Charles had bribed Spanish courtiers but had promised to offer concessions to Catholics in England if the Spanish match was secured. Charles charged Bristol with treason but Bristol offered evidence in the Lords that persuaded them that Buckingham should be the one charged with treason.

To try and stop Buckingham's impeachment, Charles rather undiplomatically implied a threat to parliament's future existence.

> Now that you have all things according to your wishes and that I am so far engaged that you think there is no retreat [from the war], now you begin to set the dice and make your own game. But I pray you be not deceived. It is not a parliamentary way, nor is it a way to deal with a King. Remember that parliaments are altogether in my power for their calling, sitting and dissolution. Therefore, as I find the fruits of them good or evil, they are to continue or not to be.

7 Charles addressing parliament, 1626. Taken from Scarboro, D.,
England 1625–1660, 2005

Charles' statement smacked of absolutism and his reliance on emergency financial measures reinforced the negative impression of Charles, which was only strengthened when he dissolved the 1626 parliament.

■ Cross-reference

For a profile of **John Eliot**, see page 24.

■ **Did you know?**

Buckingham the poisoner

A charge of the time, and to be repeated after, was that Buckingham had poisoned King James I.

Summary questions

1 List the ways in which Charles had antagonised parliament.

2 List the ways in which parliament had antagonised Charles.

3 Construct and complete a chart similar to the one shown below:

- The left-hand column shows the key events of the period.
- Indicate which of the main four themes of the period the events were related to.
- Colour-code the themes.
- Note in each column how the event relates to the theme.

Event	Finance	Foreign policy	Favourites	Religion
Tonnage and poundage	Parliament refused this			
Cadiz	Cost	War	Led by Buckingham	Anti-Catholic policy

2 Finance, failure and the parliament of 1628–9

In this chapter you will learn about:

- how finance created tension between Charles and parliament

- the impact of further foreign policy failure

- how Charles appeared to be untrustworthy

- how parliament responded to Charles' actions

- how far Charles and parliament were responsible for the breakdown of the relationship between crown and parliament.

Fig. 1 *Charles I, King of Great Britain from 1625*

The failures of the first years of Charles' reign undermined the monarch's relationship with parliament. Charles' actions in 1628 and 1629 not only added to the tension but made some MPs concerned about a more fundamental question: could the monarch be trusted to rule? As a result, in 1629, some MPs felt that they needed to make their point to a monarch who appeared to be unwilling to listen. Aware that Charles was on the point of dissolving parliament, two MPs, Denzil Holles and Benjamin Valentine, sat on the speaker of the Commons so that the sitting of parliament could not be ended. A document outlining the concerns of parliament was then read. Charles' subsequent dissolution of parliament was merely the formal ending of a relationship that had already collapsed.

The forced loan and the Five Knights' Case

Without parliamentary funds Charles resorted to a benevolence. Raised on the King's prerogative for times of emergency, payment of a benevolence was voluntary. In 1626, very few volunteered money for Charles. He therefore also imposed ship money. This was a prerogative tax raised in times of emergency, specifically war, from ports and coastal counties. The money was to fund the navy. Such was Charles' dire need, however, he called on another form of prerogative income that was easier to enforce, the forced loan.

The forced loan of 1626

Without parliamentary finance and facing war against Spain and now France, Charles called on the prerogative finance of a forced loan, equivalent to five subsidies on all payers.

The forced loan was collected in the face of opposition but the method of collection ensured that most paid. All liable were summoned to public meetings where they were individually pressed to pay. This public manner of collection made any refusal to pay a very open act of opposition. Furthermore, Charles deliberately identified himself with the forced loan, in the words of the historian Cust, making it a 'test of political loyalty'. There were, however, signs of opposition to the forced loan.

> Beware and consider what you do concerning these subsidies and loans which are now demanded of you, lest you give away not only your money but your liberty and property in your own goods. If this course be not withstood, but take effect, we shall be ourselves the instruments of our slavery and the loss of the privilege which we have hitherto enjoyed; that our goods cannot be taken from us without consent of parliament.

 Anon, 'To all English Freeholders from a Well-Wisher of Theirs, 1627'

Others were more open in their opposition.

In 1627, a Thomas Scot, MP for Kent, referred to Buckingham as the biblical figure **Agag**. Scot wrote that subjects 'may disobey and refuse an unworthy king's command and request if it be more than of duty we owe unto him. Yea, gracious subjects ought of duty in their places to discountenance and dishearten graceless tyrants that will not [punish] Agag but in his defence fall out with parliament and with loans and impositions and exalted services continue to deny right and liberty and to oppress and exhaust the people'. In the same work, Scot referred to Charles I as the biblical figure Saul. In the build up to the execution of the King in 1649 it was to be Charles who was referred to as Agag.

Activity

Source analysis

Consider how dangerous the pamphlet (Source 1) was to Charles.

Exploring the detail

Forced loans

Forced loans were a form of prerogative income for the crown. These were not demanded very often by monarchs and normally only applied to wealthy individuals. In 1626, however, Charles I demanded that all who normally had to pay a parliamentary subsidy should contribute to his forced loan that was to total as much as five parliamentary subsidies. Many were therefore concerned that Charles was using the forced loan to collect what, in effect, was parliamentary taxation but without parliament's agreement.

Key term

Agag: from Balaam's use of the name in Numbers 24:7. Agag was the King of the Amalekites taken by Saul and, contrary to God's command, spared. Saul's disobedience was the occasion of his rejection by God. In 1628, as in 1649, the message was clear: justice on Buckingham and Charles should be executed or God's displeasure was risked.

Fig. 2 *Copy of the Death Warrant of King Charles I, c. 1648*

Some judges refused to endorse the legality of the forced loan and one of Charles' chief judges, Chief Justice Carew, was dismissed. The Archbishop of Canterbury, George Abbot, who had been appointed by James I in 1610 and was no supporter of the anti-Calvinists who Charles favoured, was suspended by Charles for refusing to license the Arminian cleric Robert Sibthorpe's sermon. This sermon not only defended the forced loan but, in effect, was propaganda using the power of the Church to persuade people that it was their duty to the King to pay.

Activity

Talking point

Why would Sibthorpe's sermon (Source 2) be useful propaganda for Charles?

> If a prince impose an immoderate, yea an unjust tax, yet the subject may not thereupon withdraw his obedience and duty; nay he is bound in conscience to submit, as under the scourge for his sin.

2   *Sibthorpe's sermon, 'Apostolike Obedience', 1627*

Across the country, 76 people were imprisoned for refusal to pay the loan. This number of open resistors was merely a reflection of wider unrest at the forced loan. Only about 70 per cent of the expected amount, £267,000, was collected.

A closer look

The forced loan

The most detailed study of the forced loan is written by Richard Cust, *The Forced Loan and English Politics 1626–28* (1987). For Cust, the forced loan was important because Charles' drive to collect it alienated some of his subjects so much that they were no longer prepared to trust the King. In his book, Cust argues that war was only partly to blame for the problems of the period and that ideological division was the root cause. Cust sees a 'principled opposition' to the crown as part of a widespread political consciousness. For Cust, there is a path of dissent from the forced loan of 1626 to parliament's attack on Charles in their Grand Remonstrance of 1641. Charles was also shown as opposed to parliament. Cust, thereby, sees the potential for two sides to conflict.

Cust also stresses how Charles was a, if not the, central problem of the period. Cust illustrates that, although Charles was a difficult man to advise, he did receive good advice. Cust shows that Charles became determined not to call another parliament unless he was forced to. Like others, Cust shows that Charles regarded criticism as a sign of disloyalty because he was 'in the grip of something approaching paranoia.' For Cust, Charles desire to ensure the forced loan was collected led many of his subjects to question their 'trust and faith in the King'.

The Five Knights' Case, 1627

In November 1627, five of the main forced loan resisters brought to a head Charles' imprisonment of them by claiming a writ of *habeas corpus*. Under this ancient right, they had to be tried for an offence or be released. Charles took them to trial in the Five Knights' Case. A judgement upheld Charles' prerogative to imprison, without trial, those who refused to pay.

▨ Foreign policy failure: La Rochelle

Despite this court judgement in his favour, Charles' position was worsened by the foreign policy failure of Buckingham in June 1627. As a result of his marriage to the French princess Henrietta Maria in 1625, Charles had agreed to assist the French King to crush the Protestant rebels, the Huguenots, at La Rochelle. For this marriage, he received a payment, dowry, of £240,000. In 1627, the policy of aiding the French crown was reversed through Buckingham's attempt to relieve the Huguenots of La Rochelle. England was now at war with Spain and France. Buckingham's force landed on the island of Rhé, just off La Rochelle.

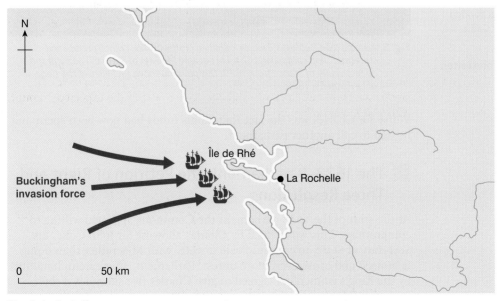

Fig. 3 *La Rochelle*

Fig. 4 *Triple portrait of Cardinal Richelieu, c. 1642*

When the French troops withdrew into the stronghold of St Martin, Buckingham laid siege. After months of deadlock, a direct assault failed when the scaling-ladders were too short! The reversal of the policy towards the Huguenots was also rendered nearly useless by the fact that the King of France, Louis XIII, and his chief minister, Richelieu, had made peace with their Protestant subjects, the Huguenots.

During the years 1624 to 1628, 50,000 men had been part of the forces under Buckingham. It has been estimated that nearly a third of these died. 7,833 soldiers went under Buckingham to Rhé. 2,989 returned. In this number was one John Felton.

Cross-reference

For information on another **foreign policy failure**, this time at **Cadiz**, see page 16.

For more information on **John Felton** see page 25.

Fig. 5 *Armand Jean Duplessis, Duc de Richelieu (1585–1642). French prelate and statesman, and cardinal in 1624. He became Minister of State to Louis XIII and de facto ruler of France from 1629. This painting shows Richelieu at the siege of La Rochelle, 1628*

Worse for Charles was the fact that all his funds had now been spent and he had to call another parliament.

The 1628–9 parliament: the Petition of Right and Three Resolutions

At the start of the 1628 parliament the Commons appeared willing to compromise. This was helped by Charles allowing Sir John Coke, his Secretary of State, to communicate directly with MPs rather than doing it himself and cause even more unrest. Parliament, after careful handling by the King's councillors, agreed to give Charles five subsidies if their grievances were addressed:

- The illegality of extra-parliamentary taxation, i.e. tonnage and poundage.
- Billeting. Troops raised for war in Europe were billeted on local populations in the south west. They had to house and feed the soldiers, which is why billeting was sometimes known as free quarter. Promised future payment often did not materialise.
- Martial law. In order to stop the soldiers billeted in the south west from becoming completely out of control, martial or military law had been imposed. Military rule that overruled all other law smacked too much of absolutism for many of the gentry.

The other remaining grievance was imprisonment without trial, which related to those who had been imprisoned for opposing the forced loan. Although the Five Knights had been released in 1628, the Commons' opposition became bitter with the revelation of Charles' actions in relation to the Five Knights' Case.

Charles claimed that the judgement in the Five Knights' Case had declared that he had the right to imprison people for 'reasons of state', what he considered to be for the safety of the kingdom. The Five Knights' Case judgement, however, was not a *general* right for Charles to imprison without showing good reason but only in that *particular* case. It became known, however, that Charles had allowed one of his leading legal officers, his attorney-general Heath, to falsify the legal records in the Five Knights' Case judgement to state that the King had a *general* right to imprison people without the need to show good reason. In theory, with this judgement, Charles could arrest anyone without indicating any reasons and not need to put them on trial. Any critic of the King, let alone opponent, would therefore be in very real danger of disappearing into the Tower of London simply when Charles felt like it.

Fig. 6 *Sir Edward Coke (pronounced 'Cook') (1552–1634) was an early English Colonial entrepreneur and jurist*

In response to the Five Knights' judgement, MPs were united in demanding action to prevent anything like it happening again.

Extreme MPs like John Selden and Sir John Eliot now considered a Bill of Rights. This would be a document that would state the rights of subjects that the King could not overrule. Parliament however proceeded with the less aggressive Petition of Right, which was mainly drafted by Sir Edward Coke.

Talking point

Concerning the Five Knights' judgement, the MP Sir Benjamin Rudyerd claimed, 'This is the crisis of parliaments. By this we shall know whether parliaments will live or die.'

1 What does Rudyerd's statement mean?

2 Is it a reliable view of the 1628 parliament?

Challenge your thinking

Divide the class into two groups. Construct an argument for and against Britain introducing a written constitution. Debate the issue.

John Eliot

Eliot (1592–1632) emerged alongside Edward Coke and Thomas Wentworth as the leading critic of Buckingham, and thereby Charles, in the parliaments of 1625 to 1629. Involved in the presentation of the Petition of Right and Three Resolutions, Eliot was regarded as going too far by many MPs and as one of the leading 'fiery spirits' by Charles. In 1629, Charles put him in the Tower of London and left him there until he died in 1632.

Edward Coke

Coke (1552–1634) was a lawyer and MP who stood against what he regarded as the early Stuarts' drift towards absolutism. Coke had a wealth of experience as Commons' Speaker, Attorney General, Chief Justice but also through his written legal 'Reports'. The key for Coke was the Common Law, which limited the authority of the monarchy. Coke influenced the Commons' Protestation of 1621, the 1625 limited vote of tonnage and poundage to Charles I and opposed the forced loan. After helping to draft the 1628 Petition of Right, Coke retired.

The supporters of the Petition of Right regarded it as in the tradition of the Magna Carta. England had no written constitution, the documented rules by which a state is run, and still has no written constitution. Only in the years 1653 to 1659 under Oliver and Richard Cromwell has England been governed by a written constitution. The unwritten constitution of England, sometimes referred to as the 'ancient constitution' was a mixture of the parliamentary laws, documents like the Magna Carta, the Common Law, as well as tradition and custom. The disadvantage of the unwritten constitution was that it was open to interpretation, but this was also its advantage. In a society that valued consensus, the ability to interpret the constitution in different ways enabled compromise to be achieved as both king and parliament had, as the ruling elite, a vested interest in working together rather than risk undermining their authority over society by becoming divided.

Fig. 7 *Written constitution*

Fig. 8 *The unwritten constitution*

The Petition of Right was a response to the concern that Charles could not be trusted to rule by the unwritten constitution. For MPs like Coke, Charles' actions in the years 1625 to 1628 had shown that his powers needed to be bounded and this required some written definition to the unwritten ancient constitution. There were four main points to the Petition of Right that indicated MPs' concerns:

1 Parliament had to consent to taxation.
2 People could only be imprisoned if just cause was shown.
3 The imposition of martial law on the population was illegal.
4 The imposition of billeting on the population was illegal.

Charles accepted the Petition on 7 June 1628 under threat of further parliamentary proceedings against Buckingham and because he was desperate for parliamentary funds for his foreign policy. Charles' first reply to the Petition did not, however, use the traditional form of assent to bills that denied the Petition the force of law. The Commons insisted

Fig. 9 *English printing workshop*

on the correct response and, as Charles needed them to vote five subsidies, he finally gave the conventional, and therefore legal, assent to the Petition. The damage, however, was already done. Charles' handling of the Petition of Right once again raised the more fundamental question as to whether he could be trusted.

With their answer to the Petition of Right secured, the Commons turned to consider the state of the kingdom, Buckingham's role, as well as religion and foreign policy. Eliot in particular was virulent in his attack on Buckingham who Coke denounced as 'the cause of all our miseries'. In a Remonstrance, a written attack, of 17 June 1628, Buckingham's foreign policy failure was attacked. A week later the Commons had to issue another Remonstrance as Charles had continued to collect tonnage and poundage that they had declared went against the Petition of Right. Parliament's deliberations were cut short, however, when the Commons' sitting was temporarily suspended by Charles the next day and, in doing so, he claimed his right to collect tonnage and poundage.

During this break in the sitting of parliament, on 23 August 1628, the Duke of Buckingham was assassinated by John Felton, a disgruntled soldier.

Fig. 10 *John Felton, assassin of George Villiers, Duke of Buckingham, 23 August 1628*

Buckingham's assassination, 1628

On the morning of the 23 August 1628, Buckingham was preparing to leave his quarters at the Greyhound Inn in Portsmouth. The lower rooms were crowded with people. As Buckingham was bidding farewell to one of his colonels the assassin, John Felton, leaned over the colonel who was bowing to the Duke and stabbed Buckingham in the left side of his chest. Buckingham pulled the knife out shouting 'Villain' and reached for his sword. As he started to give chase to Felton however, Buckingham collapsed. He was laid on a table and a search commenced for Felton who using the crowd had fled into the kitchens. Those searching for Felton suspected he was an agent of the French King, Louis XIII. As a result, as they ran through the inn they cried that they were looking for 'A Frenchman! A Frenchman!' At this, Felton came forward to proclaim, 'I am the man', and was seized.

Buckingham's body was transferred to London. Charles had to forego his desire for making Buckingham's funeral into an expensive spectacle, being made aware of the continuing financial problems he faced and the possibility of protests. In the end, on 18 September, a torchlit procession with armed men stationed along the route took Buckingham through London to Westminster Abbey.

Felton, a professional soldier, was a lone assassin. He felt he should have received a promotion to captain and had also been plunged into debt by the delays in pay. Felton had stitched a paper with the reasons for his action into his hat, no doubt assuming that he himself would have been killed on the spot and thus have no time for justification. Felton claimed that Buckingham was 'cowardly, base, and deserveth not the name of a gentleman or soldier'. Felton admitted his guilt and was hanged at Tyburn the traditional execution place of traitors. His body was taken by cart to Portsmouth where it was hung in chains outside the town.

News of Buckingham's assassination was accompanied by public rejoicing. Bonfires were burnt across England in celebration.

Charles blamed the assassination of his favourite on parliament for their portrayal of Buckingham. For some historians this was a turning point in Charles' reign, as the King withdrew even further and became closer to his French Catholic wife, Henrietta Maria, which in the long term was also to have damaging political consequences. Even in 1625, in an anonymous pamphlet entitled *Seven Problems Concerning Anti-Christ*, Henrietta Maria was attacked because of her Catholicism. The author expressed concern that Charles would succumb to the influence of his Catholic wife for 'Egyptian darkness proceeds from anti-Christ's enchantments, to hold Pharaoh still in hardness of heart'.

The 1629 parliament

The 1628 Petition of Right failed to address two fundamental points of disagreement between Charles and parliament:

1 It did not explicitly mention the customs duty, impositions, or tonnage and poundage. As a result, Charles claimed he had not surrendered his rights to collect these.

2 Charles' open favour to anti-Calvinists. In the summer of 1628, William Laud (see page 51) was appointed as Bishop of London and Montagu was appointed to Chichester. Charles was clearly indicating his continued support for Arminianism, which many regarded as a form of Catholicism.

Furthermore, the question of trust was raised again by the fact that the printed version of the Petition of Right when it appeared contained Charles' first unconstitutional answer alongside his second answer. Charles had told the royal printer to do this and ordered the statute number to be defaced, further throwing doubt on the legality of the document. When this all came out in parliament in 1629, it raised the question again as to whether Charles could be trusted to rule by the ambiguity of the unwritten constitution. If Charles could not be trusted, did there need to be some more formal means of limiting his powers that could be enforced?

Despite Charles' obvious dishonesty, there were still moderates who wanted compromise. It was Charles' refusal to compromise that played into the hands of more radical MPs like Eliot and Selden. In the Commons on 2 March, the Speaker, the King's representative in the house, was forcibly prevented by the MPs Denzil Holles and Benjamin Valentine

 Activity

Talking point

As a class, discuss the following:

'Buckingham was the scapegoat for, not the cause of, the King's problems.'

 Activity

Talking point

In pairs, discuss why the issue of trust was so important in the relationship between crown and parliament.

from reading the royal order to be suspended until the Commons had indicated support for the Three Resolutions. The Three Resolutions expressed opposition to the collection of tonnage and poundage without parliamentary approval and to Arminianism. Charles' response to the actions of the MPs was to dissolve parliament two days later.

More formally, in response to the Three Resolutions, Charles issued a Declaration.

 Activity

Source analysis

What view of parliament is suggested by Charles' Declaration of March 1629 (Source 3)?

These provocations of evil men (whose punishments we reserve to a due time) have not changed our good intentions to our subjects. We do here profess to maintain the true religion and doctrine established in the Church of England without any backsliding to Popery or division. We do also declare that we will maintain the ancient and just rights and liberties of our subjects. Yet let no man hereby abuse that liberty; nor misinterpret the Petition of Right by interpreting it to allow a lawless liberty. For as we well maintain our subjects in their just liberties, so we do and will expect that they yield to our royal prerogatives.

3 *Declaration of Charles I, March 1629. Taken from Daniels, C. W. and Morrill, J. (eds.), Charles I, 1988*

Fig. 11 *Sir John Eliot, imprisoned in the Tower of London for opposing King Charles I*

More directly, after dissolving parliament Charles had his leading opponents including Sir John Eliot, Denzil Holles and Benjamin Valentine arrested for treason. Holles left for exile while both Valentine and Eliot were put on trial and incarcerated in the Tower of London. Both refused to bend to the King's will. Valentine remained in the Tower until 1640. Eliot died in the Tower in 1632 and Charles refused to release his body for burial to his family.

By 1629, it would appear that there was a serious breakdown in the relationship between crown and parliament, one apparently confirmed by the following 11 years of personal rule and the outbreak of civil war in 1642. It would be wrong, however, to judge the early years of Charles' reign in the context of the outbreak of civil war in 1642.

One of the great mistakes in analysing any historical development is to assume that events proceed evenly along an unbroken line. That there is abundant evidence of widespread opposition to the crown in 1626 and 1627 does not necessarily mean that this opposition was maintained in the years immediately following.

4	*Coward, B.,* ***The Stuart Age****, 1994*

The three Parliaments of 1625–9 represented a range of frustrations rather than an organised resistance. They also demonstrated the limits of the powers of Parliament. There was much outspoken criticism of royal policies, but no unity of criticism. Some MPs were anxious about the Crown's religious and foreign policies, others with the legal basis of the financial measures. There was little that men such as Coke, Wentworth and Eliot shared beyond a detestation of Buckingham and the belief that the misgovernment of the present was best put right by their own entry into office.

5	*Morrill, J.,* ***Stuart Britain. A Very Short Introduction****, 2000*

Activity

Thinking point

Read Source 5. Take notes, in bullet-point form, as if you had to give a report to Charles I indicating why he need not worry too much about his situation in 1629.

Table 1 *Totals of public and private acts, 1604–29*

Session	Public	Private	Total
1604	33	38	71
1605–6	27	29	56
1606–7	13	20	33
1610 (1)	24	42	66
1610 (2)	0	0	0
1614	0	0	0
1621	2	0	2
1624	35	38	73
1625	7	2	9
1626	0	0	0
1628	8	19	27
1629	0	0	0

Information from Smith, D. L., ***The Stuart Parliaments, 1603–1689****, 1999*

Statistical analysis

Study the statistical information listed in the chart on page 29. What might it suggest about the nature of the 1620s relationship between crown and parliament under James compared to Charles? Write your response in bullet-point form.

- A session was a continuous sitting of a parliament. Thus in James I's first parliament of 1604 to 1611 there were five sessions.
- A public act was brought by the crown, i.e. government.
- A private act was brought by an MP and was usually based on their local concerns.
- An act was a law agreed, voted for by parliament, and then confirmed by the monarch.

■ A closer look

The 1620s

There are differing interpretations of the nature of the 1620s. One argument is that in the 1620s a crisis caused long-term problems that contributed to the outbreak of civil war in 1642. This crisis was part of an on-going struggle between crown and parliament for power, i.e. an ideological struggle between the prerogative and privilege. A contrasting argument has put been put forward that there was no fundamental crisis in the 1620s and no ideological struggle, but that a number of practical problems caused tension between crown and parliament but had no real impact in 1642.

If the Parliaments of the 1620s were not the scene of a power struggle between 'government' and 'opposition', if they were not polarised by ideological disputes why did they generate so much ill-will? There appear to be three important answers to this question. The first, and fundamental, reason has been called the 'functional breakdown' of English administration: the straining of the links between central and local government, which meant that the King was constantly unable to collect an adequate revenue. He was therefore forced to resort to methods of revenue collection which only increased the collectors' unpopularity. The second was the Duke of Buckingham. The third reason, bred from the other two, is the pressure of war on the English administration. Because the wars of the 1620s were so unsuccessful, it is too readily forgotten that they were seriously intended, and prepared for on such a scale as to create a severe administrative burden. It was this burden of war, imposed on an administration already in a state of functional breakdown by the Duke of Buckingham that brought relations between central and local government, and hence between Kings and Parliament, to the point of collapse. The crisis of 1626–8 was the result of England's administrative inability to fight a war.

6   *Russell, C.,* **Parliaments and English Politics 1621–9***, 1979*

■ Activity

Talking point

As a class, discuss the following question:

To what extent was the growing tension between Charles I and his opponents during the 1620s a 'breakdown of communication' as argued by Conrad Russell or a 'fundamental ideological divide' as argued by Richard Cust?

Before discussing this, one half of the class should write arguments in support of Russell's contention while the other half writes arguments in support of Cust.

The extent of ideological division has been underplayed in some of the recent accounts of the period. In particular the marked stress on the need for consensus and harmony has been taken to imply an absence of division or concern with matters of principle. To judge by the Forced Loan this would be a mistake. It forced into the open a distinction between what has been identified as two separate and conflicting themes within the political thought of the early seventeenth century. One emphasised the absolute and unlimited extent of royal power, while the other stressed that this was bounded by common law and the law of nature. These themes were normally able to coexist because of the general desire for unity and the readiness of contemporaries to paper over their differences. However, when a crisis arose which touched on basic liberties, then inevitably the conflicts were brought to the surface; and in the circumstances of the loan they were exacerbated because they came to be identified with differing views of the nature of true religion.

| 7 | Cust, R., *The Forced Loan and English Politics 1626–8*, 1987 |

Activity

Source analysis

Explain how far Source 7 differs from Source 6 in relation to the causes of tension between crown and parliament in the 1620s?

Activity

Revision exercise

1 Add to your chart from Summary question 3 at the end of Chapter 1. At the bottom of your chart insert a 'Total' row, indicating the number of times you have highlighted this column for the events listed, as in the example below.

Event	Finance	Foreign policy	Favourites	Religion
Tonnage and poundage	Parliament refused this		38	71
Cadiz	Cost	War	Led by Buckingham	Anti-Catholic policy
Total	7	8	12	4

2 For the column you have highlighted the most, write an argument as to why this factor was so important in the deterioration of the relationship between crown and parliament.

3 Add to your lists from Summary questions 1 and 2 at the end of chapter 1 of how Charles and parliament could be considered responsible for the breakdown of the crown–parliament relationship. Based on your completed lists write:

   ▪ one A4 side on how Charles was responsible for the breakdown of the relationship with parliament

   ▪ one A4 side on how parliament was responsible for the breakdown of the relationship with the crown.

Learning outcomes

Through your study in this section you will have gained an understanding of Charles' personality and style of rule, and an insight into the causes and nature of the deterioration of the relationship between crown and parliament in the years 1625 to 1629. You should be able to explain the role of religion, foreign policy, finance and favourites in the years 1625 to 1629, and have an understanding of the responsibility of Charles and parliament for the breakdown of the relationship between crown and parliament.

AQA Examination-style questions

Read Sources A–C below.

In four short years the trust between the Commons and their king had been dissolved never to return. Money and parliamentary privilege were symptoms and not the cause of the breakdown. The underlying causes went deeper. The Commons saw the king pursuing policies in religion, foreign affairs and finance which required explanation if they were ever to command widespread support. Many of the policies favoured by Charles reversed the practice of several decades, especially friendship with Spain and Arminianism. Great tact was needed in the management of these policies, but there was no effective management of parliamentary debates provided by the court. Money was requested, but the reasons for the crown's pressing financial requirements were not spelt out.

A   *Brice, K.,* **The Early Stuarts, 1603–1640**, *1994*

By 1629 the political climate had already changed considerably in the four years since his accession. Charles' policies and style of government had alienated a significant number of his subjects and raised fundamental legal, constitutional and religious issues. Unlike his father, Charles' behaviour tended to divide rather than unite the political elite, with the result that he and many of his subjects increasingly mistrusted each other.

B   *Smith, D. L.,* **A History of the Modern British Isles**, *1603–1707, 1998*

Although Charles made some effort in 1625–26 to revert to a more traditionally Protestant foreign policy, it proved to be of little political advantage. Richelieu's peace with the Huguenots reduced Charles' scope for playing the role of the 'godly prince'. In the 1626 Parliament Charles proved to have little new to offer, and his most urgent plea, now against a background of recent failure, was again for money. The Crown's critics in the Commons were not against giving, if they could be convinced that the cause was a proper one, in capable hands. But the Cadiz expedition had gone badly wrong.

C   *Quintrell, B.,* **Charles I 1625–1640**, *1993*

(a) How far does Source B differ from Source A in relation to the reasons for the breakdown of the crown–parliament relationship? *(12 marks)*

Below is a structure to help you answer 'comparison of sources' questions.

Planning your answer:

- Read the question.
- Read the sources carefully and note down any points of disagreement. Then note points of agreement.
- Decide how far they agree/disagree.
- Write your answer, referring to the sources throughout and supporting with own knowledge.

After you have made a comparison of the sources, you will be asked a follow-up question on the period. This is essay based but asks you briefly to incorporate information from the two sources that you have been asked about in part a) but also the third source, Source C, that will be on the exam paper. An example of such a question for this period is shown in part b).

(b) Use Sources A, B and C and your own knowledge. How important was finance as a reason for the deterioration in the relationship between crown and parliament in the years 1625 to 1629? *(24 marks)*

- List the key themes/factors of the period (one of which is specified in the question).
- List the key content.
- Order/structure the essay as a plan.

The key themes for this period are:

- foreign policy
- finance
- favourites
- religion
- Charles I
- parliament.

The key content for this period may then be listed or placed under the relevant themes.

The paragraph on parliament may include:

- tonnage and poundage
- funding for foreign policy
- attempts to impeach Buckingham
- the Petition of Right
- the Three Resolutions.

The paragraph on religion may include:

- Charles' Arminiamsm
- Henrietta Maria
- Montagu
- York House Conference.

3 Charles and his court

In this chapter you will learn about:

- how the personal rule has been seen

- the nature of the personal rule in the wider context of the period 1625–42

- how and why Charles shaped the court

- how Charles' court was a reflection of the nature of the personal rule

- how art can be used as a historical source.

Fig. 1 *Charles I*

The centre of politics in Stuart England was the court. The importance of the court only became more pronounced in a time of personal rule, when the monarch ruled without parliament. The court was a reflection of the style of the monarch. To some, Charles' court appeared not only absolutist but Catholic. As the centre of the kingdom, Charles' court also appeared to be shaped in the image of what the monarch wanted the kingdom to be. In 1997, the historian Young argued that although 'historians appreciate how important order was to Charles, they have not gone very far in analysing how his behaviour was typical of a controlling personality. Charles exercised enormous self-control and tried to control his external surroundings with the same rigour.' Understand Charles' court and it is easier to understand Charles and the nature of his personal rule. It is also easier to understand why others in the political nation were concerned that Charles was an absolutist and a Catholic.

The nature of the personal rule

The basic definition of the personal rule is that Charles ruled without parliament.

> Charles' non-parliamentary rule was 'personal' not only in his direct control of government but in the extent to which that government was conducted in private meetings in which the King gave verbal orders for action to be taken: it is this aspect of his rule that makes it so peculiarly difficult to establish degrees of responsibility for policy decisions.

 Atherton, I. and Sanders, J. (eds.), **The 1630s. Interdisciplinary essays on culture and politics in the Caroline era**, 2006

Activity

Source analysis

According to Source 1, what makes it difficult to decide how far Charles was responsible for the policies of the personal rule?

To understand the personal rule and the period 1625 to 1642, there also needs, however, to be some consideration of the 'nature' of the personal rule. Historians have interpreted the period in different ways.

Historiography of the personal rule

Historiography is how different historians have written about the past. The period 1625 to 1642 has created many arguments among historians. The reason for this is that the English Civil War is one of the key events of our past. Explaining why civil war broke out in 1642 has been a key question for historians. Explaining the outbreak of civil war has not only led to very different interpretations, but has coloured how the whole of Charles' reign is viewed.

The three key interpretations have been generally labelled, Whig, Revisionist and Post-revisionist. These can be summarised:

- Whig – that some form of conflict between crown and parliament was very likely, if not inevitable, as parliament sought to limit the powers of the crown. In this sense, there was an ongoing ideological struggle between crown and parliament since the imposition of feudalism in 1066 to the triumph of parliamentary democracy by the end of the 19th century. The Whig view was most prevalent at the end of the 19th century, but lasted into the 1970s.
- Revisionist – this label came from the idea that historians were revising the Whig view. In general, the Revisionist view was that conflict was very much the result of short-term factors and not ideologically driven. The Revisionist view began to establish itself from 1976.
- Post-revisionist – historians who were moving beyond Revisionism and argued that, like the revisionists, the political elite strove for consensus. However, underneath this there were different ideological stances that came into the open under the pressure of practical issues like finance, religion and foreign policy. This view is still current.

These interpretations will be considered more when looking at the causes of the civil war but they have also shaped views of the personal rule.

Table 1 *Historiography of the personal rule*

Interpretation	Historian	Argument
Whig	Gardiner	Eleven Years' Tyranny
Revisionist	Sharpe	Some creative reform

Cross-reference

For more information on the
'**thorough**', see page 62.

■ Activity

Talking point

As a class, based on the material
you have covered to date, discuss
whether or not you think Charles
was aiming at absolutism.

Consider how Charles' policies
could be regarded as absolutist and
how far this was based on the policy
itself, or how some would view it in
the light of Charles' style of rule.

The Whig interpretation of the personal rule was one of an 'Eleven
Years' Tyranny', a 'high road to civil war' in 1642. Such interpretations
sometimes saw the personal rule administration as 'thorough', a time
when Charles and his ministers imposed more central authority on the
country, which led to a reaction.

The most detailed work on the personal rule, Kevin Sharpe's *The
Personal Rule of Charles I* (1992), portrayed the period in a much more
positive light than Whig views, which merely saw it as hastening the
outbreak of civil war. For Sharpe, Charles' period of personal rule was
viable and he may have continued to rule without parliament. For Sharpe,
the period was one of stability. Sharpe indicates that Charles' attempts
to deal with some of the problems that beset early modern rulers were
creative. Sharpe's work has been seen as part of Revisionism. In part,
this can be seen by his argument that in 1637 there were no signs that
England would collapse into civil war. The balance between the negative
views of the Whigs and the more positive view of Kevin Sharpe is, as ever,
somewhere in between. There is much about Charles' rule that can be
seen in a positive light, especially in retrospect, but there was much also
that was politically naive and created an underlying discontent.

An issue raised by the Whigs with regard to the nature of the personal
rule was the extent to which Charles' rule can be considered absolutist.
A leading historian of the period, John Morrill, addressed the issue of
Charles I as a tyrant in 1990. He indicated that while some of those in
parliament may well have regarded this as being the case, there were
reasons why they did not articulate that belief, including:

■ the danger that by labelling the King a tyrant they were inviting more
radical solutions than they wanted
■ parliament had sought to pin the blame on evil counsellors and
particularly the bishops.

Was Charles aiming at absolutism?

The Privy Council

The Privy Council were the King's selected advisers who met in private to
shape the monarch's wishes into policy and oversee its implementation.
Without parliament, even more emphasis was placed on the role of the
Privy Council.

■ Activity

Source analysis

What does Source 2 tell you about
the role of the Privy Council and
Charles' management of it?

> During the Personal Rule the Privy Council formed the centre of
> government to an even greater degree than at other times. Charles I
> presided over Council meetings far more frequently than his father had
> done. Charles' close involvement stemmed from his wish to use the
> Council to implement a far-reaching reformation of government. He was
> single-minded in the pursuit of this goal, and impatient of any debate
> or dissent. As the decade progressed, his management of the Council
> revealed his essentially authoritarian temperament. Increasingly, the
> King turned to an inner circle of trusted advisers – led by such figures as
> Laud, Weston, Windebank and Cottington – who could be relied upon
> not to challenge his preferred lines of policy. Very often it was this group
> rather than the full Council which took the crucial decisions.

 2

*Smith, D. L., A **History of the Modern British Isles,**
1603–1707, 1998*

Table 2 *The major Privy councillors during the personal rule to 1640*

Name	Office	Date
Sir Thomas, Lord Coventry	Lord Keeper of the Great Seal	1625–40
Henry Montagu, Earl of Manchester	Keeper of the Privy Seal	1628–40
Sir Richard Weston, Earl of Portland	Lord Treasurer	1628–35
William Juxon, Bishop of London	Lord Treasurer	1636–40
William Laud, Archbishop of Canterbury	First Lord of the Treasury	1635–40
Francis, Lord Cottington	Chancellor of the Exchequer	1629–40
	Master of the Court of Wards	1635–40
Sir Francis Windebank	Secretary of State	1632–40

Another figure who should not be ignored was Thomas Wentworth. His appointment as Lord Deputy of Ireland in 1632 meant that he could not be part of the Privy Council. Wentworth's influence was lessened by his physical distance from Charles as Lord Deputy of Ireland (Chapter 5) but this did not mean, however, that his influence was not felt at the Council in London.

Fig. 2 *Thomas Wentworth, 1st Earl of Strafford*

There is a sense in which, initially, at any rate, Wentworth was indeed able to exert control over events more easily when away from court than when he was present there. Wentworth knew that he was no courtier, he lacked the courtly graces and the queen scarcely concealed her dislike of him. More importantly, Wentworth at Whitehall lacked the impact that he could make as a distant Deputy, where he was a qualitatively different minister, whose dispatches were often eagerly awaited. If Wentworth's absence from court presented his enemies with many opportunities to disparage him, it also allowed his supporters to put the best possible gloss on the absent Deputy's activities and motives.

| 3 | Merritt, J. F. (ed.), *The Political World of Thomas Wentworth, Earl of Strafford, 1621–1641*, 1996 |

The Privy Council also had committees to deal with what were regarded as the most important aspects of government, such as trade, Ireland and foreign policy. It appears as if there was a distinction between what one contemporary described as the 'common council' and the 'cabinet council', i.e. the Privy Council and those Charles took into even closer confidence and who dominated the Council committees. Until his death in 1635, Weston was one of Charles' closest advisers. The other dominant figures in the Privy Council with Charles were Laud and Juxon.

To enforce Charles' will and that of the Privy Council, there were two key prerogative courts, Star Chamber and High Commission.

The court of Star Chamber was made up of Privy councillors selected by the monarch. Charles could hold key cases in secret before the Star Chamber. The advantage of Star Chamber was that defendants could be questioned in private and fined, imprisoned or undergo corporal punishment. The court could not, however, sentence a defendant to death.

The Court of High Commission was the chief court of the Church used by Laud to enforce conformity. If a defendant was found guilty, they were sentenced by Star Chamber, of which Laud was a member also.

There were also two regional prerogative courts to impose control on the far reaches of England. The Council of the North, situated in York, dealt with the powerful families of the north. The Council of the Welsh Marches had first been conceived to protect the English borders from the Welsh but by 1625 their threat had evaporated.

The role of the Privy Council, and evidence for Sharpe's argument that the Council and Charles initiated creative reform in this period, can be seen most visibly in two areas of local government.

The *Book of Orders*, January 1631

Following harvest failures in 1629 and 1630, copies of the *Book of Orders* were sent to sheriffs for distribution to the Justices of the Peace and municipal authorities setting out the scope of the authority and duties of these local officials in executing legislation on a range of subjects, but particularly helping the poor. There was nothing new about this. The first books were issued in 1578 and there were 10 other years in which other books were issued before 1629.

It is, however, the *Book of Orders* of January 1631 that is far more important. This was designed to ensure that local government functioned

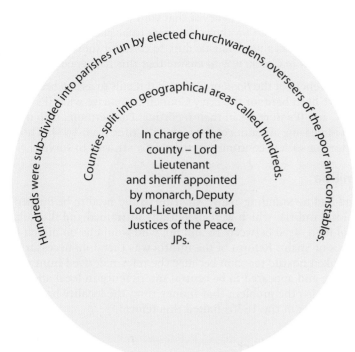

Fig. 3 *The structure of local government in England*

as it should do in terms of the gentry's local responsibilities such as helping the poor and maintaining roads. In essence, Charles' aim was to prevent social unrest and maintain order. What was new about the *Book of Orders* was the procedure laid down in them: JPs were to meet monthly in each hundred (a sub-division of a county) to supervise the work of those who administered local government: the hundred and petty constables, churchwardens, and overseers of the poor. The JPs were to send reports to the sheriffs who, in turn, reported to the assize judges on circuit, who were the direct agents of the Council commission. The JPs had to report to the Privy Council monthly. If they did not, they could be subjected to Star Chamber punishment.

Some gentry may have resented central interference in their affairs. Furthermore, if they were to undertake the tasks assigned to them, it would take time and money, which was a more serious cause of resentment. It is perhaps to Charles' credit that he wanted the gentry to fulfil their duties that befitted their place in a hierarchical society that was supposed to function on a paternalistic basis. The gentry, who had been placed by God in an elevated place in an ordered society above most of the population, had a duty to care for those less well off below them in society, especially in times of hardship.

The King, as God's representative on earth, was the head of a society that was ordered.

Within these different 'classes' there were, however, marked differences. Even among the gentry there were marked differences between the greater gentry and lesser gentry. Only those in the gentry and above had any kind of comfortable life. Much of the population lived a life where daily survival was their

Fig. 4 *The structure of 17th century society*

Fig. 5 *Sir Francis Bacon*

main consideration. It was believed that your position in life had been determined by God, but for those fortunate to be placed towards the top of society there was a paternalistic duty to consider those below them. Thus, the *Book of Orders* was to ensure that this happened.

The effectiveness of the *Book of Orders* is difficult to assess because it would have been hard for the Privy Council to manage what JPs did in the localities, and JPs were lax in their reporting. Furthermore, ship money took up increasing amounts of the Council's time from 1634. Those at the bottom of society continued in their daily struggle to survive.

The militia

England had no standing army. An army would need to be formed out of local militia, which were essentially ill-trained and ill-equipped bands of men, aged between 16 and 60, who would be no match for the forces of Spain. Reform of the militia was therefore necessary but provoked hostile reaction because the reform derived from royal prerogative and appeared to be central interference in local affairs. There was also the problem that money from the locality had to fund this. The peace of the 1630s halted this reform.

Charles I's court

In a personal monarchy, the court was the centre of power and the physical manifestation of the character and kingship of the sovereign. Charles regarded his court as a microcosm of his State – a plan for what could be achieved in the country.

> Charles' persistent effort to impose order on his own court reveals much about his mentality. He wanted to get things under control, arrange them his way. Charles subjected himself to rigid self-control. However, Charles was not just a controlled personality; he was a controlling personality. He endeavoured to impose his will on others as he had on himself, to control the external world as rigidly as he controlled his inner world. Charles tried to make the court a microcosm of what he wanted the larger macrocosm of his kingdoms to be – an ordered and virtuous commonwealth under his paternal rule.

4   *Young, M.,* **Charles I***, 1997*

The historian Kevin Sharpe has made more positive comments about Charles and his court.

> The style of Charles' court reflected the image of the king, formal and reserved. But it was not only in the sphere of morality and manners that the concern for order was revealed. The concern with order was not confined to the Court. Indeed it is important to understand that for Charles the Court was not to be, as some historians have maintained, a retreat from the world of reality, but rather a model for the reformed government of Church and state. It is in the context of these concerns, of this looking back to an idealised society of harmony and deference, that we should understand Charles' religious policy. If order was Charles' private religion, then it behoved all the more that the religion of the realm be ordered.

5   *Sharpe, K.,* **The Personal Rule of Charles I***, 1992*

Activity

Source analysis

How far does Source 5 differ from Source 4 in relation to the view they present of Charles I's court?

Did you know?

Bacon's ideas

As well as being one of James I's leading ministers, Francis Bacon was one of the leading intellectuals of the age. He believed that three inventions had brought about the New World in which he lived:

1   Gunpowder.

2   The Mariner's Compass.

3   Printing.

The apparent isolation of the court under Charles became a problem because it seemed to be based solely on Charles' supporters. Thus, it appeared to offer no link with the 'country' as a 'point of contact' in the political process.

The division between 'country' and 'court' was reinforced by Charles' orders for the gentry to spend less time in London and more time fulfilling their duties in their regions. One member of the gentry, William Palmer, was fined £1,000 in Star Chamber in 1632 for remaining in London without royal permission.

> The King observes a rule of great decorum [order]. The nobles do not enter his apartments in confusion as heretofore, but each rank has its appointed place. The King has also drawn up rules for himself, dividing the day from his very early rising, for prayers, exercises, audiences, business, eating and sleeping. He does not wish anyone to be introduced to him unless sent for.

6   *Adapted from the Venetian Ambassador's report to the Doge and Senate of Venice, 25 April 1625. Taken from Daniels, C. W. and Morrill, J. (eds.), **Charles I**, 1998*

Activity

Source analysis

1 How can Charles' ordering of the court as described in Source 6 be seen in a negative and positive light?

2 As a class, discuss how useful an ambassador might be as a source.

The political damage caused by the apparent isolation of the court was heightened by the individuals who dominated it and its visual representation. The court appeared to be dominated by Catholics or anti-Calvinist Arminians, who were regarded as nothing better than Catholics. This was a problem because Catholicism was equated with absolutism, as seen in Spain and France.

One of the main forms of court entertainment was the masque. The masque was an elaborately costumed fantasy play with dancing. The designer, Inigo Jones, produced some of the court masques. Both Charles and Henrietta Maria took part in the court masques.

The usual theme of the court masques was of disorder in the land which, at the appearance of the King and Queen, was transformed into order. In general, the masque was a reflection of the role the King felt he was fulfilling in bringing order to the country.

Fig. 6 *Henrietta Maria*

> The masque is for the monarch and about the monarch in an overt and relentless form as the king himself danced the leading part in these annual spectacles of state. Both Inigo Jones and the king made every Stuart court masque a vehicle for an exposition of the political theory of the Divine Right of Kings.

7   *Strong, R., **Art and Power**, 1984*

There was some direct opposition to the imagery of the court masques. William Prynne (page 80) produced the pamphlet Histrio-mastix in 1633. Prynne as a Puritan disapproved of women performing in plays and the index entry in Histrio-mastix, 'women actors, notorious whores', was seen as an attack on the Queen's role in the masques.

Alongside the masques, Charles' extensive art collection that he had assembled at enormous cost, together with the production of images of the King by the artist Anthony Van Dyck appeared to create the impression to outsiders that Charles aimed to be an absolutist Catholic monarch.

Because of his closeness to Van Dyck, and his highly developed knowledge of painting, it can be assumed that he exercised more control than most patrons over the images that finally emerged. Perhaps more than any of the texts produced in the 1630s, they capture the essence of how he liked to imagine himself and wanted others to imagine him.

8

*Cust, R., **Charles I**, 2006*

Fig. 7 *Title page to a vindication of the Divine Right of King Charles I, 1640*

Activity

1 Study Figure 8. What image is Charles trying to present of himself?

In relation to this, consider the following:

- Charles' stance.
- Charles' clothes.
- Charles' gaze.
- Objects in the picture.
- The background.

2 What are the uses and limits of portraits as a source for a historian?

To help you consider Van Dyck's portraits of Charles as sources, re-read Source 8.

A closer look

Van Dyck's presentation of Charles I

Van Dyck, one of the leading European artists of the age, was employed by Charles to represent him and what he believed he stood for. Van Dyck proceeded to produce numerous images of Charles as well as other courtiers in the 1630s.

Fig. 8 *Roi à la chasse*

Fig. 9 *Charles I on horseback*

The importance of conspiracy theories

The isolation of the court meant that a 'conspiracy mentality' developed. Those outside the court believed that Catholics were in control or subverting the King, whereas the King believed radical Puritans were determined to infringe on his prerogative. As there was a breakdown of communication between court and country, it was easier for members of the gentry, especially the more Puritan inclined gentry, to believe that the court was tainted by Catholicism. In turn, Charles believed that what he had witnessed with parliament in the years 1625 to 1629 was an attempt by Puritan motivated individuals to attack the powers of the crown.

By the end of the 1620s there were two structurally similar but mutually exclusive conspiracy theories, both of which alleged to explain the political difficulties of the period. The one was centred on a populist Puritan plot to undermine monarchy, the other on a popish plot to overthrow English religion and law. Both theories offered a way out of the political deadlock of 1629 by providing an explanation of conflict in terms of the activities of relatively small groups of ideologically motivated men. Thus the structure of the political system as a whole was left untouched and each side, by labelling the other as intrusive and un-English subverters of a settled system of government, was able automatically to justify its own position as the guardian of English good government. By adopting either the popish or the Puritan conspiracy as an explanation for conflict contemporaries were choosing between two very different sets of political, cultural and religious values.

Activity

Source analysis

What does Lake in Source 9 suggest was the advantage for contemporaries of adopting a conspiracy explanation for the political problems of the period?

9   *Lake, P. 'Anti-Popery: the structure of a prejudice'. Taken from Cust, R. and Hughes, A. (eds.),* **Conflict in Early Stuart England**, *1989*

Activity

Talking point

In light of the ideas about a Catholic conspiracy at court, discuss whether perception is more important than reality in shaping history.

Cross-reference

For more information on the **religious policies of the personal rule**, see pages 51–59.

Activity

Thinking point

Use the evidence of the past two chapters to write a Puritan newspaper article indicating your fears about what is happening at court to the country. In your article, try to include signs of apparent Catholicism at court.

During the personal pule, Puritan 'evidence' for a Catholic conspiracy became more centred on the religious policies of the personal rule and also on the prominence and influence of anti-Calvinist Arminians and Catholics at court. For example, it was easy for Puritans to believe that Charles would be influenced by Catholics if a range of Catholics were influential at court and thus had access to him. These included his wife, Henrietta Maria. Yet there were also other Catholics, like the first Papal Agents since 1558 to be allowed at the English court, George Con and George Panzani. Even the fact that the court dwarf, Geoffrey Hudson, was a Catholic was taken by some Puritans as 'evidence' of a wicked Catholic influence at court. Others who were not Catholic but Arminian anti-Calvinists were regarded as Catholics by some Purtians, for example the Archbishop of Canterbury, William Laud.

Summary questions

1 Describe the nature of Charles' court.
2 Explain why Charles' court raised concerns.

4

Policy: finance and religion

Fig. 1 *Charles I at prayer*

Charles' finances: revival of old methods of raising finance

Crucial to Charles' rule without parliament was raising finance, for without adequate funds Charles would be forced to call another parliament. In seeking to generate finance based on his prerogative however, Charles raised concerns that he sought to be free of parliament and establish himself as an absolute ruler. For many, such concerns appeared to be confirmed because, at the same time, Charles was enforcing Laudianism on the Church. Laudianism was seen by some as a way to introduce Catholicism, which for the majority of the English was naturally equated with absolutism. Charles' policy in finance and religion appeared, then, to be part of the construction of an absolutist Catholic State.

Key chronology

1629 £2m debt; peace with France.

1630 Peace with Spain; distraint of knighthood fines.

1633 Proclamation for nobility and gentry to return to counties

William Palmer fined £1,000 for remaining in London.

1634 Forest fines.

Ship money on coastal towns and counties.

1635 New *Book of Rates* issued.

Ship money extended inland and levied annually until 1639.

1636 Bishop Juxon appointed Lord Treasurer.

1638 Hampden's case.

1639 Growing resistance to ship money.

Attempts to secure financial independence

Finance was a real problem for Charles because of the failure to secure subsidies from parliament. By 1629, Charles had a debt of £2m. Charles' first chief financial ministers at the start of the personal rule, Weston, the Lord Treasurer, and Cottington, the Chancellor, essentially faced the same problems of raising revenue and cutting expenditure that had bedevilled previous monarchs.

Savings

Cutting expenditure was achieved chiefly by the following:

1 Peace with France (1629) and Spain (1630) through the Treaties of Susa and Madrid.

2 Weston reformed the household, the costs of running Charles' court.

Both methods had, however, negative political consequences.

War was the most significant cost for early modern governments and securing peace with both France and Spain was significant for Charles, most notably in removing any immediate need to call parliament. Charles' withdrawal from the Thirty Years' War however sat uncomfortably with many, particularly the Puritans, who regarded the destruction of Catholicism as a crusade. Many in England looked more to the victories of the Protestant Swedish King Gustavus Adolphus as a model rather than their own King.

Fig. 2 *Mary I (1516–58)*

Yet it was not only that Charles withdrew from Europe but that he appeared to favour the Catholic Spanish. The court did not go into mourning when Gustavus Adolphus was killed in 1632. The ambassadors of the Pope were allowed at the English court in the 1630s for the first time since the last Catholic monarch, Mary I, in 1558.

■ A closer look

Bloody Mary

After the death of Henry VIII's only son, Edward VI, it was his daughter, Mary, from his first marriage to the Spanish Catholic Katherine of Aragon, who became Queen as Mary I in 1553. Mary, unlike Edward, was a Catholic and she imposed Catholicism on England. Henry's Reformation had only begun in the 1530s so there were still many Catholics. The re-establishment of Catholicism also appeared to be strengthened by Mary's marriage to the man who would be the next King of Spain, Philip. Leading Protestants who would not agree to the change were publicly burnt at the stake. Their deaths were depicted in a book by John Foxe, *Acts and Monuments*, which became the second most owned book in England after the Bible and more popularly known as *The Book of Martyrs*.

Furthermore, Charles received Spanish money in the 1630s when he used his ship money fleet to protect the Spanish South American gold fleet. In 1637, Spanish troops actually landed in England to be resupplied.

Alongside decreasing expenditure, Charles sought to increase his income. This was to be done by various financial expedients based on methods the crown had used to raise money on its own authority since 1066. These methods have been termed **fiscal feudalism**.

The methods of fiscal feudalism to increase revenue

1   Collection of customs duties, including tonnage and poundage. This was only granted to Charles for one year in 1625 but he continued to collect it. In the years 1631 to 1635 this form of income brought Charles about £270,000 a year. In 1635, a new *Book of Rates* updated the amount paid on goods as a customs duty to be more in line with their market value, thus increasing the amount the crown received. By the end of the 1630s, the amount coming in from customs duties had risen to £425,000 a year.

2   Increase in the collection of recusancy fines. These were fines on those who refused, recusants, to attend the compulsory Protestant Sunday service. The most notable recusants were Catholics. In the 1620s, £5,300pa was raised through recusancy fines. In 1634, this had risen to £26,866.

3   Distraint of knighthood – a fine on anyone holding land worth £40pa or more who had not received knighthood at Charles' coronation. By 1635, Charles had raised nearly £175,000 from this.

4   Monopolies. A loophole in the Monopoly Act allowed grants to corporations, the most notorious of which was the granting of the monopoly for soap to a group of Catholics – the Popish Soap, which earned Charles £33,000.

■ Did you know?

All ships of one of the leading trading companies of this period, the East India Company, carried the Bible and *The Book of Martyrs*.

■ Key term

Fiscal feudalism: Fiscal is another word for financial. Feudalism was the organisation of society imposed on England by the Normans after 1066. Everyone owed allegiance and service to the King. The King granted land to his subjects in return initially for military service, but over time increasingly this was changed to finance. The feudal power of the crown had been moderated over time by the emergence of parliament, but the crown's prerogative forms of income still derived from feudalism.

■ Examining the detail

Book of Rates

This was a book that listed the official valuations of those items on which customs duties should be paid. The majority of items listed either paid a fixed sum or a percentage of their nominal value. As a result, this form of crown income did not stay in line with inflation. Since 1558, there had only been one revaluation in 1608 before the new book of 1635.

5 Wardships. The crown had the right to run any estate where the heir inherited under the age of adulthood, 21. During the personal rule income from wardship increased by about a third to £75,000 a year.

Fig. 3 *The unpopular 'Popish soap'*

In 1628, Charles appointed a Commission for Defective Titles to raise fines in three particular areas:

1 Forest fines – fines for any land owner said to have encroached on to areas of royal forest. Using rather dubious maps and documents, Charles imposed fines on major landowners. In total, however, forest fines only raised £38,667 at a political cost of alienating landowners.

2 Land titles – those who rented land from the crown but lacked a clear title to the land or could not prove continuous occupation for the previous 60 years were fined.

3 Enclosure fines – those who had illegally enclosed, closed off, common land.

There were also other fines, such as the fine of £1,000 levied on William Palmer for not leaving London despite the orders for the gentry to return to their localities to fulfil their duties. By exploiting his income, Charles had raised his annual income over the period of the personal rule from £600,000 to £900,000. Yet, Charles was still in serious financial problems. He had to spend anticipating his income coming in. His failure to repay debts had destroyed the chief financier of the crown, Burlamachi, by 1633. His chances of securing more credit were therefore doubtful. Charles thus needed peace if he was to avoid calling parliament.

Despite savings and increased revenue, Charles undertook no major reform of his finances that would have truly established him as financially independent of parliament and thus with the real potential to be absolutist.

The king himself had no stomach for the action that would be needed for systematic innovation. In 1635 he appointed as treasurer the unimaginative Juxon rather than the far more dynamic Wentworth. Accordingly, the later 1630s saw little further reduction in the debt; instead the king limped along by courtesy of the customs farmers. He was regularly anticipating, spending in advance. His mixed priorities were indicated by his spending on art and the plans to rebuild Whitehall. In 1640 only his servants would lend to him. Charles' finances were not sound enough to give him much safety in the troubled Europe of the 1630s.

1   *Hirst, D.,* **England in Conflict, 1603–1660***, 1999*

A closer look

The lack of fundamental reform to the crown's finances was not just a problem for Charles I. Elizabeth I (1558–1603) had not updated the sources of income and with a sustained period of inflation the weakness in crown income was exacerbated. Major reform was needed but it was safer politically for monarchs to organise their finances in the short term than undertake financial reforms, which by definition would mean dealing with the vested interests of the political nation represented in parliament. That the situation was so bad was recognised by James I's first chief minister, who had also been chief minister under Elizabeth I, Robert Cecil. In 1610, he started negotiating with parliament a major reform of the crown's finances, the Great Contract. In return for an annual grant from parliament of £200,000 and the removal of debts of about £600,000, the crown would give up some prerogative income. Both crown and parliament felt they had too much to lose in such an agreement and reform was never attempted again under James. It took civil war and the establishment of republican rule (1649–60) after the execution of Charles I in 1649 for real changes to be made to the finances of the State. With the restoration of monarchy under Charles I's son, Charles II, the crown finances essentially resorted to

Fig. 4 *Elizabeth I (1533–1603)*

their traditional short-term methods. It took another revolution, the Glorious Revolution of 1688–9 when Charles I's second son, James II, was removed because of his Catholicism and absolutist tendencies and replaced with the Dutch, William of Orange (William III) before real reform of the crown's finances took place that made the monarch reliant on parliament. It is in this context of 1558 to 1689 that Charles I's failure to reform the financial situation should be considered. In this context, his financial achievements were significant, although they cannot be divorced from their political consequences.

Some historians have clearly seen Charles' methods of raising finance as an attempt to establish absolutism.

Charles initiated a new phase in the struggle by attempting to turn England into an absolutist class-state through forced loans and various forms of extra-parliamentary taxation, which fell primarily on the English labouring and parliamentary classes. This bold, absolutist project was by no means a moribund feudalism.

2

Holstun, J., ***Ehud's Dagger. Class Struggle in the English Revolution***, 2000

 Activity

Talking point

Based on the language of Source 2 and the title of the book, discuss what interpretation of the period the author might be trying to put forward.

The form of income that appeared to give Charles most scope to exploit was ship money. Ship money was a prerogative form of income levied in times of emergency to support the navy. In October 1634, ship money was levied on coastal towns and counties. In August 1635, it was extended to inland counties and levied annually until 1639. Ship money raised an average of nearly £200,000pa, the equivalent of three parliamentary subsidies. Until the autumn of 1638 there was a collection rate of at least 90 per cent, a remarkably high return for this period and higher than Thatcher's Poll Tax of the early 1990s. Even the collapse in payment after the Scottish Rebellion and Hampden's case should be set in context. Ship money was not a tax but a rate. It was costed for a specific purpose of funding the navy year on year. The historian Kevin Sharpe has shown how the amount requested was significantly scaled down before, in its final year, being scaled up again to £210,400. Charles and the Privy Council did not expect to collect all of this but probably calculated that even a smaller percentage of this large rate was as useful as the high percentages they had collected when they had scaled down the rate. On the surface, ship money could be judged a financial success.

Ship money

> The great success story was ship money. It was not until 1639 and 1640 that the collection of ship money collapsed. Before Hampden, there were almost no objections to the levy on legal or constitutional grounds. Complaints were confined to rating disputes; protests were limited to unfair assessments.

3   *Sharpe, K., **The Personal Rule of Charles I**, 1992*

The debate about the success of ship money is focused around the real financial benefits the crown accrued from the rate against the discontent it caused, whether expressed or unvoiced. In the 17th century the majority of those liable paid taxes due to fear of punishment but also acceptance of the monarch's powers. Questioning the monarch's power would undermine the whole political system. Concern could be voiced in parliament. Without parliament, there was less scope for the grievances of the political nation to be expressed and this potentially led to the build up of unrest.

> What is difficult to determine is the extent and seriousness of the opposition to ship money before 1638. Opposition on constitutional grounds was not very apparent before that date, and between 1634 and the end of 1638 90% of the tax was paid. Perhaps, though, the lack of both vocal, principled opposition to and non-payment of ship money should not be equated with its general acceptance. In the absence of sessions of parliament there was no forum for anyone to express constitutional disquiet without exposing themselves to royal wrath. Even so, there are indications in Cheshire and Kent that ship money was discussed as an attack on parliamentary liberties.

4   *Coward, B., **The Stuart Age**, 1994*

In 1634, ship money was levied, as tradition, on coastal areas. As England was not at war it was debateable whether this could be justified as a time of emergency. The miserable state of the English navy did mean, however, that there was a serious weakness to address. The navy was also needed to counter the threat of pirates. It must also be said that the money raised through ship money was allocated to improve the navy. The extension of ship money in 1635 to cover all of England was novel but could be justified on the basis that defence was an issue for the whole country.

> Ship Money would become reviled as one of the most notorious impositions ever laid on the country, a classic case of arbitrary and overbearing government, but it was originally introduced as a response to the widely acknowledged neglect of the navy. Initially, only the coastal counties were required to supply a ship or pay the equivalent sum. So Charles was able to defend his imposition of ship money without parliamentary consent as legitimate, since it had been levied in defence of the realm. It was only when the levy was extended to the inland counties in 1635 that concerted opposition started to gather momentum.

5   *Schama, S., **A History of Britain, vol. 2, The British Wars 1603–1776**, 2003*

Activity

Revision exercise

Using Sources 3–5, create a chart listing the evidence that would suggest ship money was a success and the evidence that might indicate that it created problems.

Source	Positive	Negative

Attempts to reform the Church and the aims and policies of Laud as archbishop

Charles' favour to the anti-Calvinist Arminians was most visibly illustrated by the promotion of William Laud (Table 1).

Table 1 *The growing influence of William Laud*

1624	First appointed Bishop of St. David's, in remote west Wales, by James I at the prompting of Charles and Buckingham
1625	Laud preached to the opening of Charles' first parliament. Promoted from Bishop of St. David's to Bishop of Bath and Wells, as well as Dean of Chapel Royal.
1626	Appointed to the Privy Council
1628	Promoted to Bishop of London
1633	Promoted to Archbishop of Canterbury

Fig. 5 *William Laud (1573–1645)*

With Laud's promotion to Bishop of London in 1628 and then to the highest position in the Church, Archbishop of Canterbury in 1633 at the death of the Calvinist George Abbot, it is perhaps more proper to use the term 'Laudians' for the anti-Calvinists that had increasingly come to dominate the Church from 1625.

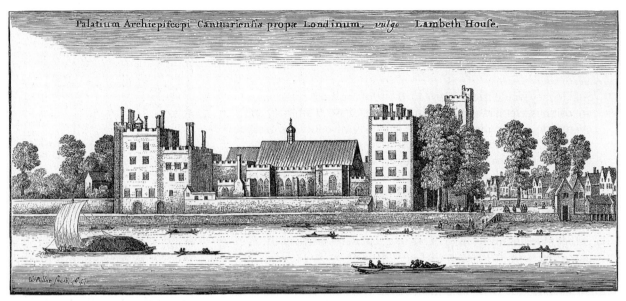

Fig. 6 *Lambeth Palace, London, the residence of the Archbishop of Canterbury*

Even before 1633 Laud's influence had outstripped his official positions in the Church as Charles chose to ignore those like Abbot whose religious persuasion was out of favour. Abbot had been appointed by James I in 1610, but in 1621 he was forced into semi-retirement, partly as James showed increasing favour to anti-Calvinists, but also because the archbishop had killed a gamekeeper with a cross-bow while he was out hunting. Abbot's isolation became pronounced under Charles I. From 1633, however, Laud could more formally impose his anti-Calvinism on the Church.

> The bishop of Canterbury departed this life on Mundaye last in the morning and he made a profession of his faith a little before his death which was that he did abhorre the religion of papists in his hart and that in his conscience he did esteeme this pope to be the greatest Antichrist that ever was. It is thought that discontent did hasten his death in regarde that the king, by meanes of the bishop of London, did urge him to approve. I am confident that we shall enjoye better tymes.

6   *A letter from a Catholic at Charles' court, 9 August 1633, Camden Society*

> Laud, lord of London, is nominated and elected already. This wilbe a great strengthening of the Arminian party against the puritans, and will make a great change generally ere long to the better, the king inclining wholly that way. It is generally thought that the times will every day grow better and better for Catholickes.

7   *A letter from a Catholic at Charles' court, 16 August 1633, Camden Society*

What was Laudianism?

Laudianism was not a coherent group with a set of beliefs. Two issues can be highlighted at the heart of Laudian anti-Calvinism:

1   Anti-predestination.

2   Less emphasis on the Bible and preaching, with more emphasis on ritual and ceremony.

The principal obsession of Laud was the emphasis which was being placed by many English bishops on the Calvinist doctrine of predestination. This struck Laud as an excessively harsh belief, the rigid acceptance of which was more likely to drive the ungodly away from the church than to attract them towards it. It was far better, he thought, to emphasise the totality of Christ's redemption so that every person would recognise that he had an opportunity of achieving his own salvation if he was guided by the word of God.

8

*Canny, N., **From Reformation to Restoration:
Ireland 1534–1660**, 1987*

The real problem was that there was a general Calvinist consensus. Charles, by siding with Laudianism and attempting to impose a new, more restrictive uniformity, broke this consensus and thereby united most Protestants, no matter their differences, against him.

James I had attempted to construct a unified Church based on a small number of key doctrines, in which advancement was open to a wide range of protestant opinion and from which only a minority of extreme puritans and papists were to be excluded. Charles I, by contrast, regarded the Jacobean achievement of unity as illusory, for it had undermined uniformity of worship and doctrine and permitted the emergence of a popular puritan threat to monarchy. Vigilant government in Church and state was necessary to cauterise this malignancy. Consequently order and obedience, authority and deference, replaced flexibility and accommodation as the hallmarks of Caroline policy.

9

*Fincham, K. and Lake, P. 'The Ecclesiastical Policies of James I and
Charles I.' Taken from Fincham, K. (ed.), **The Early
Stuart Church, 1603–1642**, 1993*

Fig. 7 *Title page of Leviathan by Thomas
Hobbes*

The measures of Laudianism

The phrase 'beauty of holiness' is indicative of what was most notable of the impact of Laudian changes to the decoration and appearance of churches. This, of course, had most impact in the churches controlled by Puritans who favoured the most plain churches. Figure 8 shows the most visible changes brought about by Laudian anti-Calvinism.

Communion table moved and railed off as an altar in the east end of the church

Increased emphasis on ceremony

Decoration

Use of music in services

Ministers wearing vestments

Removal of the gentry's ornamental pews

Fig. 8 *Laud's emphasis on outward forms*

Revision exercise

Using Source 10, list all the ways in which Charles I's religious policy could now be considered positive.

On the surface, the religious policy of the personal rule was eminently reasonable. Charles and Laud were appalled by the deteriorating physical condition of the churches. They launched a campaign to repair and adorn them. They were worried, too, by the extent to which the laity had gained power to appoint and support many of the clergy (through the purchase of impropriations). They tried to remedy this by making the clergy more financially independent of lay control. They thought that respect for the clergy had declined. They sought therefore to enhance the status of the ministry and the power of the church hierarchy, particularly the authority of bishops. They thought the actual form of worship in the church had become too lax and disorderly. They tried therefore to impose higher standards, reduce lectureships and sermons, enforce the official liturgy, and generally restore the splendour and ceremony of the church service, what Laud called the 'beauty of holiness'.

10   *Young, M.,* **Charles I**, *1997*

Most contentious of the Laudian measures was the moving of the plain communion table from the nave, the centre, to east end, then covering it in embroidered cloth and railing it off. Charles, typically, did not supply a real justification for this. For Puritans, such physical changes were elements of superstition and use of idols that they considered part of Catholicism.

Charles I's reign proved yet again that one man's godly devotion could be another's blasphemous transgression. In the cultural wars of Caroline England, preceding the actual fighting of the 1640s, few topics were potentially as divisive as the positioning and treatment of the furnishings for holy communion. Tables and altar rails stirred some people to veneration while incensing others to violence. Liturgical trappings and equipment came to encode alternative visions of community, worship, and godly devotion.

11   *Cressy, D.,* **Travesties and Transgressions in Tudor and Stuart England**, *2000*

The main strands of the altar policy derived from Laud's obsession, like Charles, with seemliness and order. In part, they were responding to reports such as the following witnessed in a London church:

A woman dandling and dancing her child upon the Lord's holy table; when she was gone I drew near and saw a great deal of water upon the table; I verily think they were not tears of devotion, it was well it was no worse.

In practical terms, the altar policy would involve the following:

- The communion table would be aligned north-south against the far east wall of the church, where the Catholic altar had been.
- The chancel, where the altar would stand, would be raised by some steps.
- This chancel area would be separated from the rest of the church by a rail.
- The altar would be covered with a decorated embroidered cloth.

The altar policy as a form of Catholicism was merely reinforced by the fact that the increased emphasis on ceremony was repetitive being centred around the catechism from the Prayer Book. The cathechism was a list of set responses that were recited at various points in the service, again mirroring what happened in Catholicism. For Laud and Charles, this all had the benefit of conformity and order. For Puritans, all of this was moving away from what they regarded as central, preaching with focus on the Bible as the word of God.

Such measures as moving the table and establishing it as an altar were coupled with a campaign against unlicensed preaching. Laud had preaching limited to Sunday mornings and evenings. Puritan preaching was also limited by a direct legal attack in 1633 on the **Feoffees of Impropriations**.

The attack on the Feoffees should be seen in the context of Laud's overall aim to restore the power and authority of the Church, whether the bishops, clergy or courts. Restoration of Church lands and Church control over clergy appointments both helped this. In a similar vein, the removal of pews that had been put into some churches by some gentry to emphasise their social standing in the community was another mark of emphasising the power of the Church over the laity.

Another measure that antagonised the Puritans was the re-issuing of the *Book of Sports* in 1633. James I had produced the *Book of Sports* in 1618. This was in response to Puritan-dominated areas, particularly in Lancashire, where pressure was put on the population to keep Sunday, the Sabbath, for God. The *Book of Sports* outlined a range of sports and activities, including morris dancing, that people could do after attending the compulsory Sunday morning service to counter this Puritan pressure. Furthermore, it was to be read from the pulpit so it was clear to everyone in the community. For Puritans, this was an attack on their Sabbatarianism, that Sunday was for worship. Laud's re-issuing of the

Key term

Feoffees of Impropriations: mainly Puritans who from 1626 had raised money to control the appointment of clergy to parishes to establish Puritan preaching. Laud had the Feoffees banned and the parishes they had owned were taken over by the Church.

Fig. 9 *Puritan satire on William Laud*

■ Key term

Visitations: involved bishops visiting and reporting on the parishes in their areas. This meant that any nonconformists, those who did not conform to the rules of the Church, could be dealt with.

■ Exploring the detail

Presentment bills

These were reports made by churchwardens but sometimes by clergy, at regular visitations of the archdeacon, detailing failings in church buildings, conduct of clergy, and conduct of parishioners.

Book of Sports in 1633 was in response to reports that Puritans in Somerset were trying to enforce observance of the Sabbath. As in 1618, it was compulsory for the clergy to read the book from the pulpit. If they failed to comply they could be expelled from their parish or imprisoned. Laud's introduction of the *Book of Sports* should be seen in the context of the other changes imposed on the Church that Puritans would have objected to.

For these measures there was enforcement through **visitations** and the ecclesiastical courts.

The focus in the instructions for the visitations was particularly on the physical aspects of the churches and the performance of the minister. These were further reinforced by the archdeacon's checks on what happened in parishes and on a much more regular basis by the reports of the churchwardens in each parish, which can be seen in Presentment bills.

A lot still depended, however, on the bishop and the local vicar and gentry of the area in how far Laudian commands were implemented and enforced.

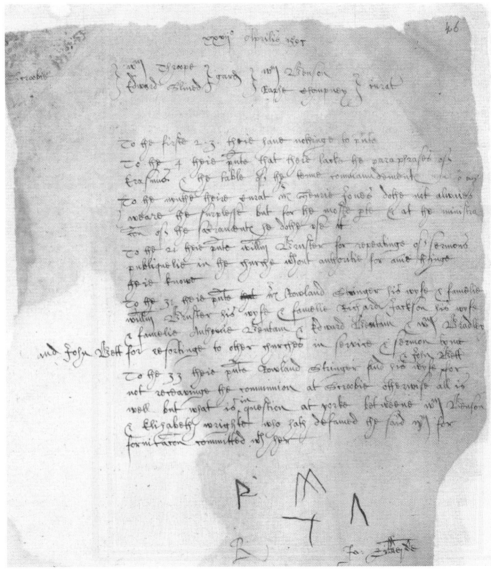

Fig. 10 *Presentment Bill*

A closer look

The problems of enforcing conformity in the localities: a Nottinghamshire parish

No matter how ordered Laud and Charles wanted the Church, in many parishes the vicar may have been the only one who shared their concerns. This can be seen from the Presentment bills that survive for the Nottingham parish of Attenborough. In 1641, one Gervase Dodson, a Nottinghamshire Laudian vicar presented one of his own churchwardens in a Presentment bill, Richard Wright, for various offences including, 'misdemeanours in his carriage when he is gone with drink, as very often he is, and his uncivil, rude and barbarous language which he often uses in public, both against his minister and against Mr Combes the Register of this Court, and against the Court itself'. Dodson, however, had also presented previous churchwardens, Thomas Cooke and Thomas Keywood for allowing the people of Chilwell in Attenborough parish to be absent from church. They were also presented for Attenborough church, 'because the vestry is decayd, & the dore into the Chancell downe, whereby the Church lyes open; & yet they doe not cawse repayre thereof, nor prsent the same'. Dodson further presented the churchwardens 'because they suffer the people (in Contempt of my admonitions) to Cary themselves unreverently in the church; some sleepinge continually, others readinge privatly unto themselves, in the tyme of prayer & sermon; other nether kneelinge at Confession, nor standing up at the Creed, nor at any tyme once openinge their mouthes, either in singing to prayse god or to saye, Amen; nor to joyne wth the minister in the saying of the lords prayer'.

Fig. 11 *Henry Ireton*

Dodson, despite his attempts to remodel the parish along Laudian lines, was faced by the apathy and sometimes hostility of most of the local population. The records show that physical changes were made to the church but the evidence of the Presentment bills would indicate that very little progress was made in winning the 'hearts and minds' of his parishioners. What did not help Dodson's campaign was that the dominant figures in Attenborough were the Puritan Ireton family, the leading member of which in the late 1630s was Henry Ireton. By 1649, Henry Ireton, with his father-in-law Oliver Cromwell, were the two men who did most to bring about the public execution of Charles I.

Cross-reference

For more information on the **growth of religious opposition**, see pages 69–73.

Naturally, as the Laudian anti-Calvinists became more entrenched in the Church as the 1630s progressed, the Puritans felt more threatened and some reacted because they felt Laud's enforcement left them little option.

Activity

Talking point

As a class, discuss whether Charles or Laud was directing religious policy.

■ Key chronology

The major religious issues of the period

1633 Laud made Archbishop of Canterbury.

At Laud's instigation, Exchequer abolishes the Feoffees of Impropriations because of their Puritan sympathies.

Prynne's Histrio-mastrix.

Re-issue of *Book of Sports*.

St Gregory's case.

Irish Convocation adopts Thirty-nine Articles.

1636 Scottish canons promulgated.

1637 Trial of Prynne, Bastwick and Burton.

Bishop Williams fined for attacking Laud's altar policy (July).

Introduction of the *New Prayer Book* in Edinburgh.

1638 Lilburne's trial; National Covenant drawn up.

Hamilton negotiates with Scots covenanters; withdrawal of Prayer Book and call of Scottish parliament and General Assembly, which abolishes episcopacy.

1640 Canons

Activity

Source analysis

What does Source 13 suggest about the role of Charles I in the religious reforms of the period?

Laud's ideas were not particularly novel in themselves. What was new was the fact that Laud – with Charles I's strong support – tried to ensure that the entire nation conformed to his preferred style of worship and wished to suppress alternatives. Reforms were accompanied by an aggressive assertion of the authority and status of the clergy. Clergy were appointed to secular offices on an unprecedented scale. Moreover, the Laudians had acquired a virtual monopoly on senior Church offices. The Laudian reforms proved intensely controversial. Many found 'the beauty of holiness', with its emphasis on ceremony all too reminiscent of Catholicism. The fact that his reforms coincided with a remarkable resurgence of Catholicism at court confirmed for some that Laud would 'unlock the door to popery'. There is little doubt that by the later 1630s Laud's reforms were widely and deeply unpopular, and this hostility took both overt and covert forms.

12   *Seel, G. and Smith, D. L., **The Early Stuart Kings, 1603–1642**, 2001*

With regard to the measures of religious reform, there has been some debate about the exact roles of Laud and Charles. Historians have different opinions of the roles of Charles and Laud. Davies and Sharpe both argued that Charles was the real initiator of change with Laud largely content to act as his master's servant. The image of Laud as an evil counsellor was a consequence of his trial. They see Laud as an essentially conservative figure intent on achieving uniformity through persuasion rather than compulsion. For Davies and Sharpe, it was Charles who gave anti-Calvinist policies their cutting edge. In contrast, Fincham and Lake have argued that Sharpe and Davies have based their view on Laud's own defence at his trial and that Charles and Laud were actually a 'practised double act'.

The new authoritarianism and the drive for uniformity owed at least as much to the king as to Laud and his fellow bishops. Charles's support for the Arminians was based less on a preference for their doctrine than on a growing hatred of puritans, who he thought were bent on subverting his own royal authority. Church and state, he believed, needed a parallel assertion of discipline and hierarchy. Convinced that kingship itself was sacramental in character, he sensed a strong affinity between the reverence, ceremony, and mystery with which the Arminians sought to endow religious worship, and the deference and ritual with which he surrounded his own presence.

13   *Woolrych, A., **Britain in Revolution, 1625–1660**, 2002*

Contemporary views of Laud

Laud hath traitorously endeavoured to alter and subvert God's true Religion by law established in this realm; and instead thereof, to set up Popish Superstition and Idolatry.

14   *Impeachment Articles against Laud. Taken from Daniels, C. W. and Morrill, J. (eds.), **Charles I**, 1998*

Clearly, as these comments come from the later impeachment charges against Laud, they are by nature negative. Laud presented what he believed in a very different fashion. For him, what he had tried to do was logical.

> The Protestants did not get that name by protesting against the Church of Rome, but by protesting against her errors and superstitions. Do but remove them from the Church of Rome, and our Protestation is ended, and the separation too.

 *The Works of William Laud, vol.2, [a Relation of the Conference between William Laud and Mr Fisher the Jesuit, 1639]. Taken from Daniels, C. W. and Morrill, J. (eds.), **Charles I**, 1998*

The reality of Laud's position was less important than what these contemporaries believed. Their perception of what Laud was doing and his influence at court was more important as it became the reality to which contemporaries reacted.

> He is the Sty of all Pestilential filth, that hath infested the State and Government of this Commonwealth: Look upon him in his dependencies, and he is the only Man, the only Man that hath raised and advanced all those, that together with himself, have been the Authors and Causers of all our Ruines, Miseries, and Calamities we now groan under.

16 *Harbottle Grimston's speech in the Commons, November 1640. Taken from Daniels, C. W. and Morrill, J. (eds.), **Charles I**, 1998*

What made perceptions of Laud and Laudianism more distorted was that Charles had cut himself off from many in the political nation.

> A contemporary caricature of Laudianism was formed. His attempts to reform the Church came to be seen as signs of encroaching Catholicism. Laudianism was seen as a source of theoretical support for the claims of royal absolutism. If the contacts between the court and the parliamentary classes which had been maintained in the 1620s had not been cut in the 1630s, might one side have appreciated the common ground it had with the other? Anyway, the fact is that the Caroline court, instead of being a forum in which royal policies could be explained and the views of the political nation listened to, became increasingly alien. Some even became convinced that there was a Popish Plot at court, centred on Henrietta-Maria.

17 *Coward, B., **The Stuart Age**, 1994*

In 1640, **convocation** published **canons** that codified Laud's measures.

The key canon required all clergy to agree to not altering the government of the Church 'by archbishops, bishops, deans and archdeacons, etc., as it stands now established'. This *et cetera oath* was seen as final proof that Laud wanted to bring in the Pope. By 1640, however, the authority of Laud, and Charles, was collapsing.

 Activity

Talking point

Discuss why contemporaries' views of Laud differ.

 Key terms

Convocation: the term for a meeting of clergy, which met at the same time as the parliament. There were two convocations, one for Canterbury, the most important, and the other for York.

Canon: church laws passed by convocation.

Activity

Write a justification as a Puritan indicating why your experiences and what you know of the imposition of Laudianism since 1633 have made you decide to emigrate to North America.

Summary questions

1. Explain why Charles needed to raise money on his own prerogative.

2. For each of the methods of raising income listed in this chapter, note why it may have raised concerns among the parliamentary class.

3. List all the changes to the Church made in this period and note why each raised concern.

4. Why do you think religious changes were so contentious in the 17th century?

5. If Charles I's religious policy stemmed from a genuine religious belief, was he right to implement the changes he made or should he really have thought about religion more politically?

5

Ireland and Scotland under Charles

THOMAS WENTWORTH, EARL OF STRAFFORD.

OB. 1641.

Fig. 1 *Thomas Wentworth, 1st Earl of Strafford*

In this chapter you will learn about:

- Wentworth's policies in Ireland
- the role of Wentworth in England in 1625–32 and 1639–40
- Charles' aims in Scotland
- how Charles ruled Scotland
- the nature of Charles' religious policy in Scotland.

The idea of 'thorough' and the role of Thomas Wentworth in Ireland and England

Charles' rule was not confined to England. It could be argued that Charles' rule of Ireland and Scotland was even more problematic and that the tensions created in his other kingdoms would, ultimately, have dramatic damaging consequences on his rule in England.

Thomas Wentworth in England, 1625–32

In the years 1625 to 1628, Thomas Wentworth, a Yorkshire MP, was regarded by Charles as one of his leading parliamentary critics. In some ways a natural ally of the monarch, Wentworth, like others, had been forced to use parliament as a means to pursue his own interests because Buckingham so dominated the court. In particular, Wentworth had lost

■ Cross-reference

For more information on the **1626 parliament**, see pages 14–16.

■ Exploring the detail

Council of the North

This was one of the prerogative courts of the crown established as a means of imposing and maintaining control of the north of England. The Council of the North, situated in York, dealt with the powerful families of the north as part of this means of control.

influence in Yorkshire to a client of Buckingham. Wentworth was in a group of critical MPs referred to as the 'Northern Men' because they represented northern areas, like parts of Yorkshire. Wentworth's standing as a leading critic of the crown is illustrated clearly by Charles' decision to select Wentworth as sheriff and thereby stop him from being an MP in the 1626 parliament. In 1627, he was arrested for not paying the forced loan but in 1628 Charles made Wentworth President of the Council of the North.

On the surface, Wentworth would appear to have switched sides and his acceptance of office may have been an issue for his erstwhile former parliamentary allies, although there was no open expression of discontent. It would be wrong, however, to think of the politics of the period in such a light. The politics and patronage of the period were fluid and there was not a set division between crown and opposition.

As Charles' representative in the north, Wentworth made himself unpopular with the northern gentry who saw him as agent of the imposition of central royal control against their interests. Indeed, Wentworth's apparent bluntness did alienate many of the important northern gentry.

In 1632, Wentworth was promoted to be Charles I's representative in Ireland, as Lord Deputy of Ireland.

The idea of 'thorough'

The Whig interpretation of the personal rule was one of an 'Eleven Years' Tyranny', a 'high road to civil war' in 1642. Such interpretations sometimes saw the personal rule administration as 'thorough'.

This was a term most strongly associated with Wentworth's rule in Ireland. The term related to the attempt to increase the royal authority through the imposition of religious conformity and the use of the prerogative courts. In Ireland, in particular, it also related to making a profit out of the country for the crown rather than incurring an expense and controlling the parliament in Dublin. Many English observers regarded it as a testing ground for policies for England.

The term 'thorough' gives, however, the impression of too much coherence, whereas government was still generally the normal ad hoc decision-making process of previous rulers. Charles had general aims but the nature of the early modern State meant there were limits to what he could achieve without the backing of the parliamentary classes, independent finances and a bureaucracy.

> It is tempting to treat the administrative activities of the king's government during the personal rule as a coherent policy of 'thorough'. It may be that Laud and Wentworth would have liked to have achieved effective paternalistic government, not by any radical departure from, but by a stricter enforcement of existing legislation and methods. However, there is little evidence that they were able to put such policies into effect in the 1630s. Rarely does it seem that Caroline government succeeded in breaking free from the normal pattern of ad hoc decision making.

1 *Coward, B., **The Stuart Age**, 1994*

The term 'thorough' for some was more appropriate for Wentworth's aims in Ireland than Charles' two other kingdoms.

In Ireland, Wentworth hoped to find 'the opportunity and means to supply the king's wants' and intended to rule in the manner in which he hoped eventually to govern England, absolutely, efficiently, and without regard to any interest but that of the crown; in his own word, 'thoroughly'.

2

Clarke, A., A New History of Ireland.
Early Modern Ireland, 1534–1691, 1976

Key chronology

1632 Appointment of Wentworth as Lord Deputy.

1633 Wentworth arrives in Ireland.

1634 Irish parliament.

1634 Thirty-nine Articles adopted by Irish convocation.

1634 Appointment of John Bramhall as Bishop of Derry.

1639 Wentworth recalled to England.

1640 Irish parliament.

1641 Irish Rebellion.

Thomas Wentworth in Ireland and England

Ireland was politically divided into the following groups:

1   Irish Catholics – the native Gaelic-speaking Irish population.

2   Catholic Old English – those descended from the original English settlers who were Catholic.

3   Protestant New English – those descended from English settlers after the Reformation who were Protestants.

4   Presbyterian Scots – predominantly based in the Plantation of Ulster in the north of Ireland.

Fig. 2 *Map of Ireland, 1616*

In the north of Ireland the policy of 'plantation' since 1608 had brought more Protestant settlers into the country but English control in Ireland was essentially limited to Dublin and the surrounding area, known as the Pale. Beyond the Pale, the Irish Catholic traditional ruling elite still controlled most of the country.

Appointed as Lord Deputy of Ireland, the King's representative in Ireland, in 1632, Wentworth stood outside the different factions in Ireland to divide and rule them. On his arrival, the fact that each group believed they were in Wentworth's favour gave the Lord Deputy the advantage of turning them against each other.

■ **Key profile**

Thomas Wentworth

Although a prominent opponent of the forced loan of 1626, Wentworth actually went out of his way to submit to the King during his confinement, paving the way for his appointment as President of the Council of the North in 1628 and Lord Deputy of Ireland in 1632. Recalled to England in 1639 to deal with the brewing crisis, Wentworth became Charles' chief advisor and was created the Earl of Strafford, Lord Lieutenant of Ireland and Lieutenant-General of the army. He advised Charles to call what was to become the short parliament (April 1640) to help him crush the Scots.

Fig. 3 *Wentworth in Ireland*

In Ireland, Wentworth aimed to:

- impose the authority of the English crown and Church on the Irish
- allow the English crown to profit from Ireland.

To help him do this, Wentworth chose some able assistants:

- George Radcliffe, Wentworth's former secretary, was brought into the Irish administration.
- Christopher Wandesford, Wentworth's cousin, stood in when the Lord Deputy was absent.
- John Bramhall, Wentworth's chaplain, appointed Bishop of Derry.
- Philip Mainwaring appointed as his secretary in Ireland.

A new *Book of Rates* was successful in raising finance for the crown from Ireland. From 1633 to 1640 it doubled customs income to £80,000pa. A fine on the city of London, the government of the capital city, of £70,000 also raised income. The city of London had a large grant of land in the north of Ireland, Londonderry. Wentworth argued that they had failed to carry out their duties there in developing the area.

The 1634 Irish parliament would see the implementation of the agenda of Charles and Wentworth.

> Wentworth assured Charles I in correspondence that he would break a hundred parliaments and make him the most absolute king in Christendom because this was precisely what Charles wanted to hear, and to be reassured by. This was as much, if not more, the language of the Personal Rule than were all the masques that emphasised harmony, unity and consensus. Moreover, Wentworth's correspondence with Charles over his plans for the 1634 Irish Parliament show just how intolerant Charles was.

3	*Milton, A. in Merritt, J. F. (ed.), **The Political World of Thomas Wentworth, Earl of Strafford, 1621–1641**, 1996*

Wentworth's policy of playing each group off against each other helped him manipulate the 1634 Irish parliament. What also helped his strategy was the prior announcement that the parliament would meet in two sessions. The first of these would deal with finance before the second addressed any grievances.

The first session of the 1634 Irish parliament voted six subsidies but in the second session there was no redress of their grievances. Immediately, Wentworth antagonised the Old English elite and Irish Catholics by not confirming by parliamentary statute the 'Graces'. The 'Graces' were an agreement that had been reached with these groups by Wentworth's predecessor in 1628. In return for subsidies of £120,000 over three years, they were granted the following concessions:

- Recusancy fines would not be levied.
- Relaxation of checks (the oath of supremacy) on Catholics in public office.
- Guarantee of land titles over 60 years old.

Plantation, the settling of Protestants mainly in the north, continued being directed at countering the influence of the Old Irish and also the Catholic Old English, the descendents of pre-Elizabethan settlers. Wentworth extended plantation into Connacht, including the Old English county of Galway. In July 1635, Wentworth personally attended meetings to establish the crown's right to disputed lands.

Personal attacks on two leading figures among the New English also alienated a group who should have been the key supporters of the crown in Ireland. Richard Boyle, Earl of Cork, was fined £15,000 by Star Chamber and Sir Francis Annesley, Lord Mountnorris was charged with treason. These were specifically selected as powerful members of the New English elite to set an example to others.

The imposition of Laudianism was also a problem in Ireland. For the Protestants in Ireland, like those in England, Laudianism was seen as too close to Catholicism. The religious context of Ireland made this more of a problem. The Protestants were in many ways a besieged minority and, thus, generally felt more threatened by the imposition of Laudianism. Furthermore, those who were 'planted' into Ireland tended to be the more radical protestants and again felt more threatened by the imposition of Laudianism.

In imposing Laudianism on Ireland, there is clear evidence of a concerted approach by Wentworth and Laud. Laud was Wentworth's chief ally at court in England and there was regular correspondence between the two men. John Bramhall was appointed in 1634 as Bishop of Londonderry to lead the Laudian anti-Calvinist changes on the ground in Ireland. In 1634, the Irish convocation adopted the Thirty-nine Articles. A new Irish Court of High Commission was established to enforce Laudianism. Other courts, like the Commission for Defective Titles and the Court of Castle Chamber, were used to recover land for the church. The attack on land rights alienated the New English in particular as the group who had benefitted most from the Reformation.

Despite all Wentworth had done, another Irish parliament in 1640 successfully managed to produce four subsidies for Charles I. However, Wentworth's role in Ireland created tensions that, when unleashed, were to have a significant impact on the developing crisis between crown and parliament in England in 1641.

> In England and Scotland, many suspected that Ireland was being used as a laboratory to test reforms which would then be introduced on the mainland. Wentworth achieved the remarkable feat of uniting against himself hitherto mutually hostile sections of Irish society. Worst of all, by tolerating Catholicism and imposing Laudian reforms on the Church of Ireland, Wentworth left the Protestants of Ulster and the Pale feeling more and more insecure. They reacted by demanding much tougher measures against Catholics; and it was in an attempt to forestall such measures that the Catholics rebelled in 1641.

4   *Smith, D. L., A History of the Modern British Isles, 1603–1707, 1998*

In 1639, Charles I recalled Wentworth to England to help him deal with the Scottish crisis. Along with William Laud, Wentworth had become one of the 'evil counsellors' of the King who opposition were determined to remove.

Cross-reference

For more information about the clash between **crown** and **parliament in 1641**, see Chapter 9.

Activity

Thinking point

Write a report as if delivered by Wentworth to Charles on his return to England in 1639. In this report, outline the extent to which the aims for ruling Ireland were achieved by the time you left, as well as the potential problems remaining from English rule of Ireland.

The attempt to extend religious reform to Scotland

Charles' aim was uniformity and conformity across all of his kingdoms. Rather than aiming at unifying his kingdoms, Charles' priority was to impose uniformity. Though Scottish, Charles was an absentee king of his native country and his policies and style of rule alienated the Scottish elite.

Immediately, in 1625, Charles' Act of Revocation, which took land from the Scottish elite to strengthen the Church of Scotland, set the tone for Charles' approach to Scotland. The historian Wheeler explains why Charles' Act of Revocation worried the Scots.

Fig. 4 *Charles I, defender of the faith in England and Scotland*

> Charles' first step in this burst of royal reform was to revoke many titles to Scottish crown and church lands that Scottish nobles had acquired since 1540. This revocation of land titles was precedented. Traditionally, Scottish monarchs had the right to do so after their accession, as long as they did so between their twenty-first and twenty-fifth birthdays. Charles had to act fast in 1625, since his twenty-fifth birthday was approaching shortly.
>
> While there was a precedent for the revocation, the scale on which Charles revoked titles to land was new. Normally, a monarch revoked titles to royal and church land that had been obtained while that monarch was a minor. However, in going back to 1540 in his revocation, Charles expanded his claim to dispose of the property of his subjects. This startling display of the royal prerogative frightened many Scottish nobles and clergymen.

5 Wheeler, J. S., *The Irish and British Wars 1637–1654*, 2002

The immediate response to the revocation was to unite the landed community against the threat posed to their power. Such was the unity of Scottish opposition that Charles' establishment of a Committee for Surrenders in 1627 was, in practical terms, an admission of failure. The committee essentially left the process of revocation in the hands of the Scottish elite and, although the 1633 Scottish parliament ratified revocation, nothing was achieved by the crown. Indeed, the policy had failed but, worse, it had shown the limits of the crown's power in Scotland.

Policies without consultation with the Scottish elite that undermined their position and were imposed from London were unlikely to be well received. Charles merely confirmed the Anglo-centric nature of his absentee kingship by filling the Scottish Privy Council with nine non-resident English members. The men he relied heavily on for advice on Scotland, Menteith, Lennox and finally Hamilton, were also seen as too Anglo-centric, that is, more concerned with their interests in England. The revocation should have indicated to Charles the problems of imposing threatening powers on the Scottish elite. Clearer advice from a broader section of the Scottish elite would also have helped Charles not to make more mistakes.

It was the more overt aspects of Charles' religious policy in Scotland that were most contentious. Charles' aim in Scotland, as elsewhere, was to strengthen the Church financially, enhance the role of bishops and have a shared Laudian form of worship. This would be particularly problematic in Scotland. The reason for this was that Scotland was predominantly **Presbyterian**.

Key chronology

1625 Revocation

1627 Committee for Surrenders

1633 Charles visits Scotland

1636 New canons

1637 New Prayer Book

1637 Scottish Rebellion

1638 National Covenant

Key term

Presbyterianism: the form of Protestantism that had taken root in Scotland. The Presbyterian Church, or Kirk, did not have the monarch as its head, or bishops. In ideas, it was closer to the Puritans of England than the Church of England and would, like the Puritans, have regarded Laudianism as little more than Catholicism.

Fig. 5 *The Scottish Prayer Book Rebellion*

In 1626, the King issued a proclamation commanding observation of the Articles of Perth. He also included personal instructions for kneeling at communion.

In 1633, Charles visited Scotland for the first time since becoming King of England. The impression he created was not a strong one. Indeed, the very fact that it had taken him eight years to visit Scotland was a clear sign to Scots of his priorities. His coronation ceremony was also offensive to Scottish sensibilities. The traditional site for a coronation was Scone or Stirling. Charles chose Edinburgh's Holyrood Palace. The form of ceremony chosen by Charles was also seen by Scots as Catholic. The creation of a new bishopric in Edinburgh and the raising of St Giles in that city to the status of a cathedral could also have easily been regarded as Catholic by Presbyterians.

While in Scotland, Charles announced his intention of introducing a new prayer book and, in preparation for this, he imposed new canons in 1636. The key aspects of the canons were:

■ the altar had to be placed against the east wall of the chancel

■ ministers had to wear a surplice when they celebrated communion

■ a ban was placed on improvised prayer.

All of these were interpreted as part of an attempt to bring about the return of Catholicism. What made these reforms worse for the Scots was the fact that they were imposed by royal prerogative. Charles made no attempt to allow the General Assembly of the Kirk or the Scottish parliament to have any say in the canons.

In 1637, the new Laudian prayer book was introduced into Scotland. Again, Charles imposed this without any consultation with the Scottish Kirk or parliament. This was not the introduction of the *English Prayer*

■ **Exploring the detail**

Articles of Perth

The Articles of Perth were forced through Scotland's General Assembly by James I, employing all his political skill in 1618. They had five parts: kneeling at communion; observance of holy days; private baptism; private communion; and confirmation by bishops. For Presbyterians, they looked like Catholicism.

Book into Scotland but a prayer book produced specifically for Scotland. What was so offensive to the Scots about this prayer book was that for them it leaned clearly towards Catholicism. Furthermore, its imposition simply antagonised them even further.

> The king's introduction of a new book of canons in 1636, and a new prayer book in 1637, not only aroused resentment on account of its Anglicising influences, but because of its apparent and imagined connection with a popish plot at court. The new liturgy certainly was directly borrowed from England and there was a public perception that Laud was behind a scheme to restore popery to Scotland. The canons and prayer book were introduced by prerogative by a despotic absentee surrounded by popish advisors, or so it seemed.

6   Brown, K., ***Kingdom or Province? Scotland and the Regal Union, 1603–1715***, 1992

 Activity

Revision exercise

Using Source 6, summarise the reasons why the canons and the *New Prayer Book* were so controversial for the Scottish.

> Charles' actions in the first nine years as King of Scotland badly eroded the trust between the monarch and the Scottish nobility. Such trust had been an important political tool for his father, who used the nobles to rein in the power of the clergy. Charles I eventually drove the nobles to make common cause with the Calvinist ministers of the Scottish Kirk because they saw Charles' political and religious policies as two sides of a single strategy to increase the power of the crown at the expense of the traditional elites.

7   Wheeler, J. S., ***The Irish and British Wars 1637–1654***, 2002

Activity

Source analysis

Using Source 7, list the reasons why Charles I's rule of Scotland was problematic.

The introduction of the prayer book into Scotland in 1637 proved to be a turning point in Charles' personal rule.

Summary questions

1 List what could be regarded as mistakes in Wentworth's handling of Ireland?

2 Note how else Charles I could have ruled Ireland.

3 What mistakes did Charles make in ruling Scotland?

4 How should Charles I have ruled Scotland?

5 In which country, Ireland or Scotland, did Charles' rule create more problems?

Learning outcomes

Through your study in this section you will have gained an understanding of the nature of the personal rule and its reflection in the court of Charles I. You should also be able to explain how Charles raised money, the idea of 'thorough' and Wentworth's policies in Ireland. You should also have gained an understanding of the nature of the Laudian reform in England and in Scotland.

AQA Examination-style questions

Read Sources A–C and answer the questions that follow.

The king's court should be seen as an expression of his personality and capacity as a ruler and, at the same time, as a means of shaping the attitudes of his subjects. Everything that happened there provided an example to guide the nation. Charles was acutely conscious of this and devoted considerable effort to making his family and court an image of the virtue he wished to instil into his people.

 A   *Cust, R.,* **Charles I**, *2006*

Even if Charles did try to project an image enhancing his authority, the effect was not entirely what he intended. To the extent that the populace at large had any inkling of the high culture at court, they were as much disturbed as awed by it. Court culture was impressive, but it was also alien. It was continental and Baroque. By embracing the art and artists of this movement, Charles was in effect embracing the style of the Counter-Reformation.

 B   *Young, M.,* **Charles I**, *1997*

While many suspected that Charles and Laud were secret Catholics, others feared that, even if they were not, they were allowing Catholicism to creep into the Church of England and so doing the devil's work. Catholicism was becoming fashionable at Court. The Queen exercised her right to worship in the Catholic way. Nothing indicates Charles' lack of political awareness more clearly than his decision in 1637 to welcome an ambassador from the Pope, George Con, as a permanent resident at Court and allow him to become a personal friend.

 C   *Wilkinson, R.,* **Years of Turmoil. Britain 1603–1714**, *1999*

(a)   How far does Source B differ from Source A in
      relation to the culture of Charles' court?   *(12 marks)*

Look for areas of difference. Source B is not as clear as to whether court culture really had a widespread impact. In contrast, Source A does not really address the actual impact. Source A focuses on the example Charles wanted to portray of his family.

Look for areas of agreement. Both sources see that Charles was trying to shape his court to make an example to the people. There is, however, a different emphasis. Source A is more positive about Charles deliberately shaping his court and its culture, whereas Source B is not so direct.

Use your own knowledge that can be linked to the source as examples/ illustration: Source A can be linked to how Charles consciously ordered his court. This was seen as a model for the order he sought to bring to the country.

Source B can be linked to examples of the court culture, whether the art of van Dyck or the use of the masque.

(b) Use Sources A, B and C and your own knowledge. How important was Charles' court in provoking fears of his religious intentions in the years 1629 to 1638? *(24 marks)*

In part b) questions, you must ensure that you make use of all three sources. For this question, the following provides examples of how the sources may be used as part of an argument:

■ Source A can be used to comment on how the court was used by Charles as a model for the nation.

■ Source B can be used to comment on the negative impact of court culture.

■ Source C can be used to comment on the prominence of Catholics at court.

In addressing the court, you should provide examples of why it provoked fears of Charles' religious intentions. In this regard, the emphasis of Sources B and C with their focus on court culture and Catholics at court indicate examples you could use. For court culture, you could consider the art or the masque. For Catholics at court, you could refer to Henrietta Maria and the papal agents as well as other Catholics who were prominent.

The question asks for a judgement and you should, therefore, consider other things that provoked fear of Charles' religious intentions, notably the imposition of Laudianism. Was this the most important factor? Would the imposition of Laudianism have had more of an impact on a wide range of the population than the nature of the court? Did some contemporaries make a link between the nature of the court and the imposition of Laudianism?

6 The growth of opposition

Fig. 1 *Lilburne punished*

In April 1638, John Lilburne was dragged through the streets of London and whipped every three or four paces as he staggered forward. Despite being whipped, Lilburne continued to recite scripture and cried out 'Praise be given to thee O Lord for ever'. What occasioned Lilburne's punishment, but also his resolve in the face of it, was religion. Religion was central to 17th-century life and the attempts under Charles I to reform the Church through Laudianism were to provoke such strong responses. However, it also provoked a much more widespread unseen unease that only found open expression in 1640. The historian John Morrill has referred to a 'coiled spring effect' in relation to the build up of tension under Charles' personal rule, without which the crisis in the years after 1637 is inexplicable. The signs of opposition with Charles' personal rule that were part of this build up of opposition can be regarded, therefore, as representative of wider unexpressed discontent.

The vast majority of those liable for the range of fiscal feudal measures imposed by Charles throughout the personal rule paid what was demanded of them. There were two key reasons for this. Firstly, non-payment could lead to punishment by the crown, whether by fine or imprisonment. The more underlying reason for outward acceptance of the forms of fiscal feudalism was their essential legality. By their very nature, Charles had selected forms of income that were not new but traditional feudal methods by which the crown raised income. It was therefore difficult to challenge them legally, especially as all the courts were the monarch's. Concerns over such things as the methods by which the crown raised finance were also raised traditionally in parliament. It was obviously not clear in the 1630s that the next parliament would not be until 1640.

Although most people met the financial demands of Charles' methods of raising money in the 1630s, there was, if not open opposition, some grumbling. Edward Hyde, 1st Earl of Clarendon, claimed that the abuses of the Court of Wards were a reason for many siding with parliament. Charles' grant of the monopoly of the manufacture of soap to a group of Catholics was denounced as the 'Popish Soap' monopoly.

Hampden and opposition to financial levies, especially ship money

A clearer stance against fiscal feudalism came in October 1634, when the Earl of Warwick challenged forest fines in the Waltham Forest area. Warwick was powerful enough to take legal action and his stance should also be seen in the light of the stand of his close associate, Lord Saye and Sele, against the most contentious form of fiscal feudalism, ship money.

Source 1 would suggest that, on the surface, there appeared little opposition to ship money.

> All things are at this instant here in that calmness that there is very little matter of novelty to write, for there appears no change or alteration either in court or affairs, for all business goes undisturbedly on in the strong current of the present time to which all men for the most part submit. I think that great tax of the ship money is so well digested I suppose will become perpetual.

1 *John Burghe to Viscount Scudamore, October 1637. Taken from Daniels, C. W. and Morrill, J. (eds.), **Charles I**, 1998*

Most people did pay ship money. Until 1638, over 90 per cent of the amount assessed was collected.

> Ship Money did establish a new style of taxation. Where parliamentary subsidies were levied as a proportion of income and depended on individual assessments which were cumbersome to administer, Ship Money targets were set by the government as a global sum to be levied from the county as a whole. This placed the burden of collection on local justices and cost the government little or nothing. Secondly, in combination with rising custom revenues derived from growing trade, Ship Money offered a long-term prospect of real financial independence for the monarchy. Thirdly, and perhaps for that very reason, it does seem to have created serious and deep-seated opposition.

2 *Anderson, A., **Stuart Britain 1603–1714**, 1999*

Activity
Source analysis

How far does Source 2 differ from Source 1 in relation to their views of ship money?

Cross-reference

For more information on **Laud** and his **prayer book**, see page 92.

In order to fund an army to face the Scots covenanters, who rebelled against the imposition of the Laudian Prayer Book, Charles sought legal confirmation of his right to collect ship money. It was this action that brought opposition to ship money into the open. William Fiennes, Lord Saye and Sele, had opposed ship money. He had gone as far as to start legal action against the crown deliberately aiming to be the subject of a show trial about ship money. His provocation was ignored.

Key profile

William Fiennes, 1st Viscount Saye and Sele

Saye (1582–1662) was a Protestant peer involved in North American and Caribbean colonisation plans. In 1630, with Brooke and Warwick he founded the Providence Island Company to colonise a small West Indies' island. This company could be seen as a centre for a network of opposition to Charles and Laudianism. John Pym acted as the company's treasurer. Saye was one of those in England who had contacts with the Scots, recognising that their military force would lead to an English parliament. Both Saye and Brooke refused to take a military Oath of Loyalty to support Charles against the Scots. As a result, both were imprisoned for four days and then sent to their country estates. Following the short parliament's dissolution, Saye and Brooke with Pym and Hampden were briefly imprisoned and had their studies searched for documents that might show their treasonous communication with the Scots. In the long parliament, Saye generally supported the Commons' increasingly tougher line but at times did not appear to have the courage of some of his political allies. He kept contacts open with the court and when Pym brought the attainder bill for Wentworth to the Lords, Saye claimed illness and retired to his bed.

Instead, in November 1637, Charles took to court a prominent member of the gentry, John Hampden, for his refusal to pay ship money. Hampden was of significance because he was closely connected with those Charles regarded as opponents of his regime, men such as Viscount Saye and Sele, the Earl of Warwick and John Pym. The prosecution of Hampden would make the point to all that Charles' authority should be obeyed.

Key profile

John Hampden

A minor member of the Buckinghamshire gentry, Hampden (1596–1643) became an MP in 1621 when he became close to Sir John Eliot, probably Charles' leading opponent of the time. Hampden refused to pay the forced loan of 1626 and was briefly imprisoned. His uncle, Edmund Hampden, died as a consequence of his imprisonment for refusing to pay the forced loan. In 1635, he refused to pay some of his ship money assessment. Prosecuted by Charles I in 1637 for this, Hampden's trial made him a leading public opponent of the regime. He was selected to accompany Charles to Scotland in 1641 by parliament. Such had become his stature that in January 1642, when Charles marched into parliament to arrest who he regarded as his five leading opponents, Hampden was one of their number. Hampden died in battle in 1643.

Fig. 2 *John Hampden*

Arguments were put forward by Hampden's lawyer, Oliver St John, and for the crown by the Solicitor-General Sir Edward Littleton. Both were essentially moderate in their approach. Oliver St John did not deny Charles I's right to take action in an emergency or to decide when there was an emergency. What he focused on was the methods by which the call for ship money had been formed. The writ did not state that there was an emergency and the writ was issued six months before the fleet was prepared, in which time a parliament could have been called and a subsidy granted. Littleton's response to this was to concentrate on the timing, arguing that there was not enough time to call a parliament and for a subsidy to be voted. It was the junior lawyers on both sides, Robert Holborne for Hampden and John Bankes for the crown, who brought up the wider and more serious constitutional issues.

Smith, a modern historian, believes that Hampden's case did spark constitutional debate.

> Hampden's Case had raised the profound issue of whether the royal prerogative could really be both absolute and limited. Perhaps the most dangerous aspect of Charles' behaviour was that in a political culture which revered consensus, it stimulated debate. Reactions to Ship Money surely demonstrate that quietness on the surface does not necessarily indicate the existence of stability and consensus.

3   *Smith, D. L., **A History of the Modern British Isles**, 1998*

The 12 judges of the court bench were to deliver their judgements in pairs, from the most junior to the senior. Judgement in the case was therefore spread over a period of six months with later judges aware of their counterparts' previous judgements. At one point, there were five judgements in Charles' favour and only one for Hampden. In the end, the judgement was seven to five in Charles' favour.

Victory for the crown by the bare majority has often been portrayed as a moral victory for Hampden. The judgements could have clearly gone more in Charles' favour but care is needed to set the judgement in the context of how contemporaries saw it. Apart from Judge Hutton, and especially Judge Croke, those who had judged in Hampden's favour had done so on close technical reasons. Many informed contemporaries were clearly aware of the complexities of the judgements and that the seven to five majority did not mean that there were big differences of interpretation between the judges. One attorney who commented on the judgement of Judge Jones for Hampden actually felt that, in the end, Jones had supported the King. Others clearly felt the same, for the Marquis of Hamilton thought that the judgement was eight to three. It is perhaps telling that the comment of the lawyer Bulstrode Whitelocke was that it was only Croke and Hutton who actually argued against the King. Yet Hampden's case was a problem for Charles.

Hampden's case had made it more difficult to collect ship money, although once judgement had been made it should be noted that payment returned to more than 90 per cent in total. Hampden's case also raised the debate of wider constitutional issues as the opinions of the judges were widely circulated.

Activity

Talking point

As a class, discuss the usefulness of sources such as private notes or diaries, especially in the context of statements such as those in Source 4.

The King hath no prerogative but that which the law of the land doth give and allow, and therefore his subjects could not with justice be denied a trial. The Kings of this nation do in time of peace govern by their laws, in times of war by an absolute power; but the affirmation of a necessity could not be held to be one, for at home there was no likelihood of any insurrection.

4 *Sir Roger Twysden of Kent, his private notes. Taken from Quintrell, B., **1625–40**, 1993*

Cross-reference

For more information on the **Five Members' Coup** and the **Nineteen Propositions**, see pages 128 and 134.

Another contemporary comment on Hampden's case comes in Source 5, from the man who wrote the first history of the English Civil Wars, Edward Hyde, Earl of Clarendon.

The Crown and State sustained damage by the deserved reproach and infamy that attended the Hampden judgement. Parliament hath proceeded principally from their contempt of laws and that contempt from the scandal of that judgement.

5 *Hyde, E., **The History of the Rebellion**, 1888*

Fig. 3 *Edward Hyde*

Key profile

Edward Hyde, 1st Earl of Clarendon

An MP in the short parliament and long parliament, Hyde (1609–74) was involved in criticising abuses of the personal rule like ship money and Star Chamber. Hyde had a role in preparing the charges for Wentworth's impeachment but did not like the threat to episcopacy in the Root and Branch Petition. Essentially a conservative, Hyde moved over to support the King, or rather monarchy, in 1641 as the best defence of order. Hyde became the leading figure in the constitutional royalist party that sought to prevent the King taking any aggressive measures in the continuing search for settlement. Hyde opposed Charles' Five Members' Coup of January 1642 but continued to support monarchy. In June 1642, Hyde helped produce The Answer to the Nineteen Propositions, which outlined the constitutional royalist position, that monarchy was the best protector of the Church, the constitution and order.

Activity

Talking point

In pairs, assess Clarendon as a source for the personal rule.

You need to bear in mind the above Key profile and the information in Table 1 when assessing Clarendon as a source.

Table 1 *Edward Hyde, 1st Earl of Clarendon*

1629–40	Member of Devon gentry concerned about measures of personal rule but expressed no opposition
1640	Returned as MP for Saltash, Devon to the long parliament and voted with radicals such as Pym to abolish ship money and Star Chamber
1641	Voted in favour of the Act of Attainder – a legal means by which Charles' principal advisor Wentworth was executed – but was increasingly concerned by what he regarded as the radicalism of some in parliament
1642	Produced The Answer to the Nineteen Propositions for Charles I, outlining why the King should be supported
1646	Went into exile and served Charles' son, Charles Stuart
1660	After 14 years in exile, Clarendon returned to England as Charles II's principal advisor, the Lord High Chancellor
1667	Dismissed and sent into exile by Charles II
Post 1667	Constructed his history of the Great Rebellion, a history of the Civil Wars

It was the Scottish Rebellion which precipitated Hampden's case and led to more problems with the collection of ship money. As a result of the Scottish Rebellion and Hampden's case, both obvious signs of the crumbling of Charles' authority, collection of ship money in the following year collapsed from 90 per cent to 20 per cent.

Prynne, Bastwick and Burton and opposition to religious change

Before Hampden's case, there had been other signs of opposition to the personal rule, most notably to the religious changes imposed.

One of the first open signs of opposition to the religious changes imposed by Charles I came in 1633. Parishioners of St Gregory's Church in London were brought before the Privy Council by Charles I as a test case after they had challenged the moving of their communion table to the east end of the church. The moving of the communion table sometimes also meant that family pews had to be moved causing offence. The moved communion table was covered with a richly-decorated cloth that was offensive as it appeared like the Catholic high altar. Furthermore, the altar was railed off separating it from the congregation, again reminiscent of Catholicism.

St Gregory's case did not prevent others from voicing concern over the religious changes. In September 1634, Robert Heath, Charles I's own Chief Justice of the Common Pleas, was dismissed at the instigation of Laud because Laud was concerned that Heath might oppose the religious changes in the courts. Bishop John Williams was imprisoned in 1637 as a result of his published criticism of the altar policy in *The Holy Table, Name and Thing*. Williams' criticism indicates that even terminology was a source of contention. The word 'altar' was regarded as Catholic. The anti-Calvinist Richard Montagu instructed his officials in Norwich, 'we ought not to be offended at the name, thing, or use of altar'. More tellingly, in 1637, a minster commented in relation to Laud's use of terminology: 'He speaks for altars – altar! altar! altar! altar!'

There were others, notably Puritans, who openly criticised the religious changes. Laud's 'Beauty of Holiness', the decoration of churches and focus on outward forms of religion, was regarded by many as popery.

> The Church is now as full of ceremonies, as a dog is full of fleas.

6   *The Letany of John Bastwick, 1637. Taken from Daniels, C. W. and Morrill, J. (eds.), **Charles I**, 1998*

Fig. 4 *John Bastwick*

For Puritans, ceremonies were a mark of Catholicism. In 1637, John Bastwick was brought before Star Chamber for his criticism with two other Puritans, Henry Burton and William Prynne. Prynne had been before the courts in 1633 for his pamphlet Histrio-mastix. In this, Prynne, according to another Puritan, 'let slip some words tending to the Queen's dishonour, because he spoke of the unlawfulness of men's wearing women's apparel and women's men's'. This was seen as an attack on Henrietta Maria because of her prominent role in the court masques.

Fig. 5 *Henry Burton*

In 1637, Prynne, Bastwick and Burton found themselves publicly mutilated for their criticism of Laud's innovations. Fined £5,000 each, and imprisoned for life, it was the public cropping of their ears that earned the three men sympathy.

The sympathy was not so much because of the punishment but that it was inflicted on three men who were professionals, a lawyer, doctor and cleric. The numbers who had actually read their work was limited. The numbers who knew them because of their punishment was much greater.

Linked to the opposition of these three men was the case of another Puritan, John Lilburne, who had helped distribute Bastwick's work.

Key profile

John Lilburne

Lilburne (c. 1614–57) was the younger son from a Durham gentry family who went to London as an apprentice. A Puritan, he attacked the Laudian bishops in print and helped distribute the works of similar-minded Puritans like Bastwick. Imprisoned by Star Chamber in 1638, the return of parliament in 1640 saw his release. Lilburne became a Lieutenant-Colonel in parliament's Eastern Association Army alongside Oliver Cromwell. When he left the army in 1645, Lilburne returned to writing pamphlets and became a leading figure in the movement known as the Levellers who called for social and political reform.

Fig. 6 *John Lilburne, also known as 'Freeborn John'*

Like Prynne, Bastwick and Burton, Lilburne's opposition was driven by his Puritanism and, like them, he committed himself to print. In February 1638, Lilburne was sentenced in Star Chamber with printing unlicensed literature. The next month, Lilburne's punishment was carried out. Lilburne had been fined, but then, in public, he was whipped and pilloried. The brutality of the punishment is clear from the detail. Shirtless Lilburne was tied to a cart which pulled him the two miles from the Fleet Prison to Westminster. Every few paces

Lilburne was whipped. Lilburne was then put back in prison. Lilburne continued to write. He attacked his punishment in *A Worke of the Beast*. In 1639, he referred to those who had sentenced him as 'limbs of the Beast spoken of Revelation 13.2'.

The opposition of these men may have been driven by their Puritanism but Charles' changes had unsettled many others. Another sign of discontent with the Laudian Church was the high level of emigration during the personal rule.

> The Great Migration to New England coincided almost exactly with the personal rule. Between 1629 and 1640 about 60,000 made the journey. By no means all of them emigrated for religious reasons, but the high proportion who did brave such a vast and perilous change of life for the sake of their faith, and the number of ordained ministers who sailed with them, are eloquent testimony that for a significant sector of the English people the only religion permitted to them by law had become offensive to their consciences to a degree unprecedented before Charles' reign.

7 *Woolrych, A., **Britain in Revolution**, 2002*

There have been differences among historians over the impact and reaction to the Laudian changes. Whig historians saw Laudianism as having a negative impact on the Church, leading to a Puritan revolution. For Nicholas Tyacke, Laudianism also led to a reaction but it was the Laudians who were the revolutionaries because they were the minority who were breaking a general Calvinist consensus that had been constructed by Elizabeth I and James I. In considering the reaction to Laudianism and specific examples like Prynne, Bastwick and Burton, care does need to be taken to set them in a wider context. There might have been a broader sympathy for the punishment of these Puritans but, in the context of the whole population, John Morrill has pointed out that Laudianism may have been more acceptable. The majority of the population probably attended church because they had to. The intricacies of theology were of no importance to them. Laudianism with its emphasis on ceremony, visual aspects and music would have been easier to sit through than the Puritan's emphasis on preaching. The survival of the Church of England says much for the strength of style over substance.

At the root of concerns over the religious policies of the personal rule was the anti-Catholicism that was a central feature of English Protestantism, and more so for Puritans like Prynne, Bastwick and Burton.

> An irrational fear of Catholicism lay just below the surface of English society in the seventeenth century. This had little to do with the actual numbers of Catholics in the country. It had more to do with the feeling that Protestants were under threat. The most popular book at this time, apart from the Bible, was *The Book of Martyrs*. The dread that Catholics might once again seize control of England was increased by a series of alarms from the 1580s onwards, the Armada, the Gunpowder Plot, and invasion scares in the 1620s. In Charles' reign there was a new fear that Catholicism had infected the very heart of government and the idea of a conspiracy to destroy the liberties and religion of the country gained widespread currency.

8 *Brice, K., **The Early Stuarts, 1603–1640**, 1994*

Activity

Talking point

As a class, discuss what you think were the advantages of choosing emigration as a response to the imposition of Laudianism.

Activity

Revision exercise

Using the above paragraph and the information on pages 51–59 on Laud and reform, write a paragraph supporting the historian whose argument you find most convincing, Tyacke or Morrill.

Activity

Source analysis

Using Source 8, explain why anti-Catholicism was part of English society in the 17th century.

A closer look

The development of anti-Catholicism from the Reformation of the 1530s was shaped by some key events:

- The return of Catholicism under Mary I, 1553–8: with the death of Henry VIII's only son, Edward VI, the first daughter of Henry VIII came to the throne. Mary was Henry's daughter from his first marriage to the Spanish princess Katherine of Aragon. It was Henry's divorce from Katherine that had been one of the precursors of the Reformation and the establishment of Protestantism. Mary returned England to Catholicism and under her many Protestants were burnt at the stake.

- John Foxe's *The Book of Martyrs (Actes and Monuments)*: This account of Mary's burning of Protestants became the second most read book in England after the Bible, and resulted in anti-Catholicism becoming part of the English identity.

- The Spanish War: Under Elizabeth I, the Spanish threat heightened anti-Catholicism, notably at times such as the attempted Spanish invasion of 1588, the Spanish Armada.

- The Gunpowder Plot, 1605: The attempt by a group of Catholics to blow up King James I and parliament vividly illustrated the real threat from English Catholics no matter how small their numbers.

Fig. 7 *Actes and Monuments by John Foxe*

- The Thirty Years' War, 1618–48: the religious war in Europe had some impact on English opinion. The major defeat for the Protestants in 1620 at the Battle of the White Mountain raised the spectre of Catholic invasion, which was repeated at various times throughout the war.

Activity

Revision exercise

Copy the spider diagram below, add extra circles branching out from the outer circles to explain the rise of anti-Catholicism since the Reformation.

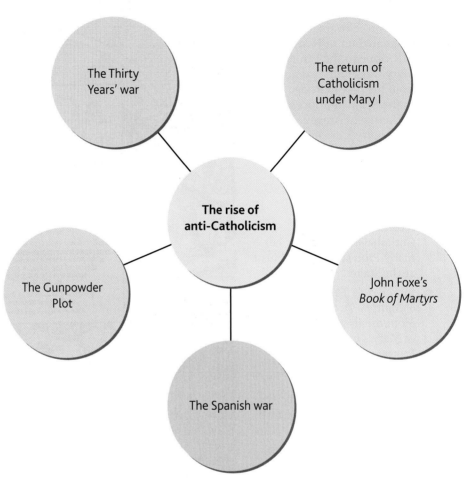

Fig. 8 *The roots of English anti-Catholicism*

What was perhaps most significant about reaction to Laudianism was not so much the open opposition of more committed individuals such as Prynne, but the perception of Laudianism as part of Charles' personal rule. Not only was it what Charles did, but it was also the way he did things that created the impression for many that he was undermining the Church and State, at worst he was aiming at Catholicism and absolutism. For many, they reacted to Charles' rule in the light of their perception of what he appeared to be doing.

Cross-reference

For a profile of **Mary I**, see page 47.

Activity

Revision exercise

Construct a risk assessment chart for Charles I. Summarise the threat (high, medium or low) posed by the examples of opposition in this chapter.

Example	Date	Nature	Numbers involved	Outcome	Threat
Hampden	1637–8	Finance Constitutional	One – but indications of others linked to Hampden, e.g. Saye and Sele	Victory in court for Charles but raised debate across country	Medium– evidence that ship money was still collected until Scottish Rebellion

Summary questions

1 Explain why Hampden's case was important.

2 'Charles did not need to worry about the verdict in Hampden's Case.' Explain why you agree or disagree with this statement.

3 Why do you think there are more examples of opposition to Charles' religious policies than there are to his financial policies?

7 The crisis of the personal rule

In this chapter you will learn about:

■ the nature of opposition to the regime

■ the nature of the Scottish Rebellion and the response of Charles I.

Key chronology

1637	Trial of Prynne, Bastwick and Burton.
	Bishop Williams fined for attacking Laud's altar policy.
July	Introduction of the *New Prayer Book* provokes riot in St Giles' Cathedral, Edinburgh.
	Hampden's case starts.
1638	National Covenant drawn up.
	Judgements in Hampden's case.
	Lilburne's trial.
	Hamilton negotiates with Scots covenanters – withdrawal of the *New Prayer Book* and call of Scottish parliament and General Assembly. This abolishes episcopacy. Charles resolves to quell covenanters by force.
1639	First Bishops' War – pacification of Berwick.
	Growing resistance to ship money.
	Wentworth arrives in England – created Earl of Strafford (1640).
1640 **13 April – 5 May**	Short parliament.

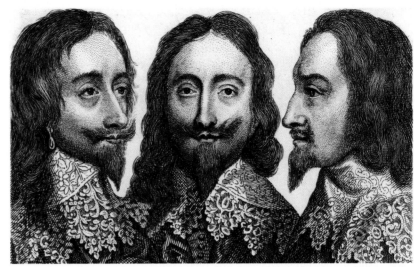

Fig. 1 *King Charles I*

As Charles prepared to send an English army north to subdue rebellion in Scotland, one of his chief ministers, Windebank, believed the crisis would not last long.

> The work will be done very shortly; for I think there will be no man so mad when the King's Army is in the field to hazard both their life and money. Although there are many that will say well to thee now but, when they see an Army in the field they will turn their coat and will be glad to come in to the King.

In fact, the Scots were soon to invade England and occupy Newcastle.

The crisis of 1637 and the general reasons for opposition to the regime

1637 was the turning point of Charles' reign. Hampden's case, the trial of Prynne, Bastwick and Burton all happened against the backdrop of rebellion in Scotland. In looking at the general reasons for, and the nature of, opposition to the regime both open opposition and underlying discontent must be considered, as well as the links between the two.

Activity

Revision exercise

Using the following information in the rest of this chapter, construct a chart showing examples of opposition. Indicate how the opposition was limited but also why it was potentially dangerous for Charles.

Example of opposition	Potential danger for Charles	Limitations to opposition

What is clear about the examples of open opposition is that they were predominantly a reaction to Charles' imposition of Laudianism. Those who were prepared to be open in their opposition were clearly the more committed and thus numbered many Puritans. Such was the strength of their faith that they were courageous enough to risk all the punishments the crown could inflict on opponents. Later, Gerrard Winstanley commented: 'You know that while the King was in the height of his oppressing power, the people only whispered in private chambers against him: but afterwards it was preached upon the house tops, that he was a tyrant and a traitor to England's peace and he had his overturn'.

Did you know?

Gerrard Winstanley and the Diggers

After the Civil War and execution of Charles I in January 1649, Winstanley was leader of a radical movement referred to as the Diggers. In April 1649, they set up a commune where all shared the land, near Kingston upon Thames, but it was suppressed by some of the local gentry.

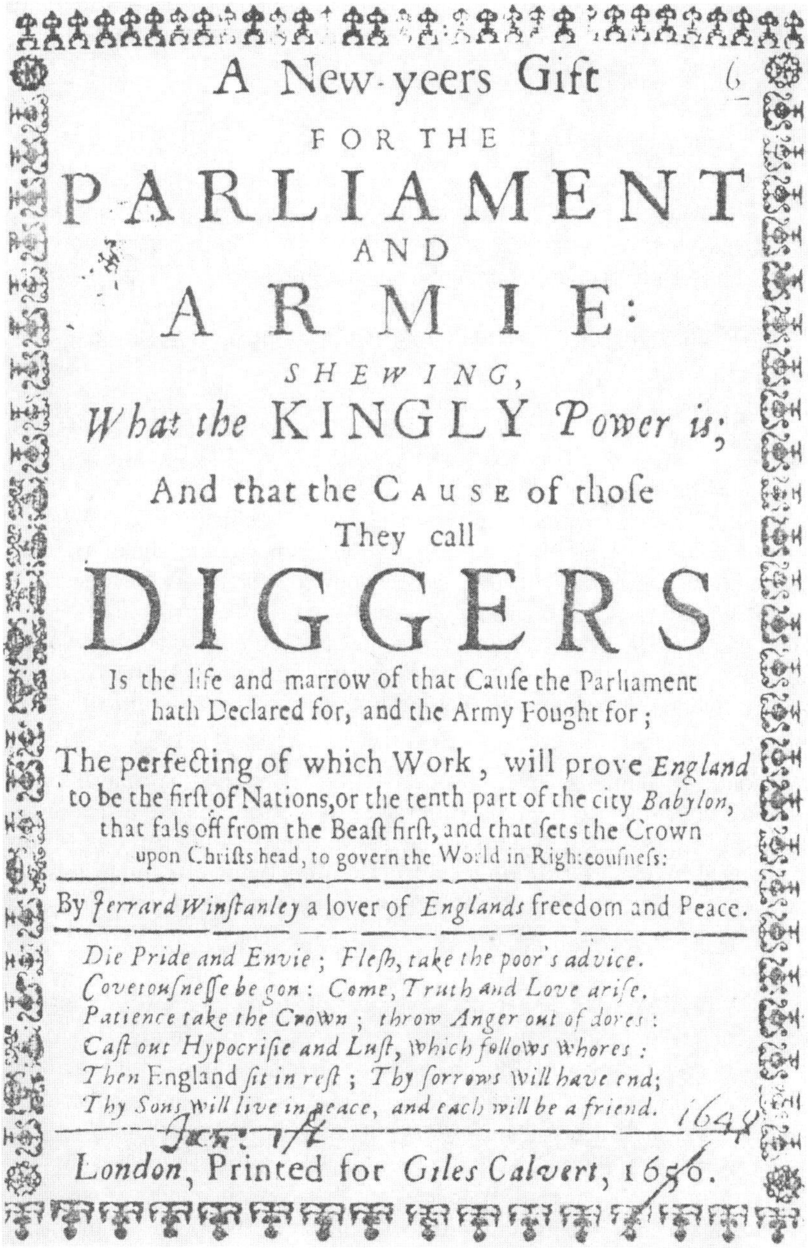

A New-yeers Gift
FOR THE
PARLIAMENT
AND
ARMIE:
SHEWING,
What the KINGLY *Power is;*
And that the CAUSE of those
They call
DIGGERS
Is the life and marrow of that Cause the Parliament hath Declared for, and the Army Fought for;
The perfecting of which Work, will prove *England* to be the first of Nations, or the tenth part of the city *Babylon*, that fals off from the Beast first, and that sets the Crown upon Christs head, to govern the World in Righteousnes:

By *Jerrard Winstanley* a lover of *Englands* freedom and Peace.

Die Pride and Envie; Flesh, take the poor's advice.
Covetousnesse be gon: Come, Truth and Love arise.
Patience take the Crown; throw Anger out of dores:
Cast out Hypocrisie and Lust, which follows whores:
Then England *sit in rest; Thy sorrows will have end;*
Thy Sons will live in peace, and each will be a friend.

London, Printed for *Giles Calvert*, 1650.

Fig. 2 *Diggers broadsheet*

All cases of open religious opposition to the regime should, however, be considered in the light of the wider underlying discontent of which they were symbolic, in addition to the well-known examples of opposition – the numerous small examples of pamphlet and manuscript attacks on the regime. In May 1629, such a printed attack was found in London and given to Laud. It read: 'Laud, look to thy self: be assured thy life is sought. As thou art the fountain of all wickedness, repent thee of thy monstrous sins, before thou be taken out of the world. Assure thy self, neither God nor the world can endure such a vile counsellor to live.'

Those of less committed faith than Puritans like Burton or Bastwick may not have been prepared to openly oppose the regime, but once the Scottish Rebellion started to clearly undermine Charles' authority, and once Charles had to call parliament, underlying discontent came to the surface.

> The widespread resentment created by Laud's influence and actions therefore helped to create opposition to the Personal Rule itself. While anger at the changes in the Church might have been limited to a Puritan minority, the fear of Catholicism and the pretensions of the Laudian clergy had a much wider impact. By 1637 there are signs of mounting discontent and a growing desire for Parliament to be called, since there was no other legal means of expressing grievances.

1 *Wilkinson, R.,* **Years of Turmoil. Britain 1603–1714***, 1999*

The underlying discontent can, however, be seen. When, in the 1970s, historians like Alan Everitt considered private sources like the diaries of some of the gentry of Kent, they clearly showed expressions of concern and discontent at the policies of Charles. What these sources also indicated was discussion among the gentry of their concerns, a network of discontent. Such concerns some of these gentry would express openly as MPs when parliament, recalled in 1640, gave them the political forum to do so.

Without a parliament, which has been described by the historian Elton as 'a point of contact' in the political process, opposition had to be expressed differently. In a society where consensus was sought and open opposition could lead to harsh retribution, evidence of underlying discontent can be seen in diaries and in the numbers of people who decided to leave England, mainly for New England.

> In the absence of parliament which was the main forum for voicing political opposition, there was very little opportunity to express any disagreement with royal policies. To do so openly, for example in a pamphlet, invited charges of sedition or even treason and the fearful penalties these entailed. The fate of Prynne, Bastwick and Burton, although an extreme example, aroused widespread revulsion. People might dislike government policies but there was no effective way of combining to express that dislike. Significantly, there was an upsurge in emigration.

2 *Brice, K.,* **The Early Stuarts 1603–1640***, 1994*

Emigration not only had the benefit of getting away from Laudianism, the freedom of North America allowed for the establishment of godly Puritan communities that they could control. Influential opponents of the regime, such as John Pym, were heavily involved in companies that promoted colonisation in New England and the Caribbean. The Providence Island Company and The Saybrooke Venture could be regarded as networks for opposition. Saye and Brooke were both godly peers and their purchase of land in North America and support for those emigrating to settle there was an expression of disgust at Charles I's Laudianism. In the meetings of these companies it is likely that discussion also centred on domestic politics. Crucially, with the crisis of 1637, company meetings could provide a good cover for the meeting of like-minded men. It is no wonder that Charles later ordered a search of the papers of men like Saye and Brooke for evidence of treason. In July 1637, as part of the imposition of religious uniformity, Laud secured the cancellation of the charter of one of the New England companies, the Massachusetts Bay company.

Fig. 3 *The Providence Island Company and The Saybrooke Venture*

Involved in both were Lord Brooke, Lord Saye and Sele, the Earl of Warwick and John Pym. Alongside these men, John Hampden was involved in The Saybrooke Venture and Oliver St John was part of The Providence Island Company. Note should also be taken of the kinship ties that bound some of these chief opponents of the regime together.

The Earl of Bedford who, in 1640, was a leading opponent of the regime, was father-in-law to Lord Brooke. When commenting on who were the leaders of the long parliament, Edward Hyde listed many of those who had been linked together in the 1630s, like Bedford, Saye and Sele, Oliver St John and Pym.

Nevertheless, despite their organisation and, at times, visible opposition to the policies of the personal rule, it could be argued that these men made little impact on the direction of Charles' policies. The clearest evidence of this is seen in early 1638. Lord Brooke and Viscount Saye and Sele were making serious preparations to emigrate to America, a most telling sign of their despair.

There could only be more widespread and open opposition through parliament. The aim of those who had concerns about Charles' personal rule was that their grievances would be addressed by a parliament. The 1640 parliament was only called, however, because Charles I was faced by a religious revolt in Scotland, and religion was clearly the core of opposition to the regime and its collapse.

Opposition to the personal rule should also be considered in the context of the years 1640 to 1642.

> Charles' programme thus proved intensively divisive and generated debate over fundamental constitutional and religious issues. Although such debate was usually covert and seldom voiced in public, it undeniably took place. It therefore seems likely that the calm of the personal rule was deceptive, and that while Charles' three kingdoms appeared quiet enough on the surface, underneath there lurked deep-rooted tensions and grievances. To many observers, and not only those who looked back with hindsight after the outbreak of civil war, the 1630s were indeed a halcyon idyll of peace and calm. Yet the same decade prompted widespread unease about Charles' kingship and generated a climate of mistrust without which the rapid breakdown of 1640–2 is impossible to explain.

*Smith, D. L., **A History of the Modern British Isles, 1603–1707**, 1998*

That MPs were generally united against the abuses of the personal rule when parliament returned in 1640 can be taken as a sign of the widespread discontent that Charles had caused among the political nation. Parliament was only recalled in 1640, however, because of what really sparked a crisis in 1637 – the rebellion in Scotland.

> The fiscal, political, religious and cultural problems of the 1630s were not unmanageable, but they belied the conceit, promoted by court conservatives, that these were England's Halcyon Days. Apologists for the personal rule of Charles I frequently asserted that England was the most fortunate of kingdoms, but this was a blinkered perception, or pride before a fall. The Caroline regime's imposition of a ceremonialist prayer book on Presbyterian Scotland in 1637 destabilized the politics of both north and south Britain. England's peaceable kingdom – once the envy of war-torn Europe – became embroiled in a British rebellion.

4

*Cressy, D., **England on Edge. Crisis and Revolution 1640–1642**, 2006*

The reaction in Scotland to the religious reform and the nature and outcome of the Bishops' Wars

England and the Scottish Revolution, 1637–40

Charles I was the cause of the Scottish Revolution. His imposition of uniformity on the Church especially alienated the Scots against bishops for, as a predominately Presbyterian nation, they had always regarded bishops with suspicion. In 1637, some bishops went into the pulpit armed when they had to read the new Laudian prayer book imposed on Scotland by Charles I.

Charles cut himself off from influential Scottish opinion and was thus less aware of, or ignored, the growing discontent. In 1639, some of the Scottish opposition claimed that Charles was a 'king far from us, in another kingdom, hearing the one party, and misinformed by our adversaries'.

A clear sign of discontent came in 1634 when many of the lords in Scotland petitioned against Charles' religious innovations. Charles rejected this completely. When Lord Balmerino tried to revive this protest, he was convicted of treason and sentenced to death. Only pressure from an outraged Scottish nobility made Charles spare Balmerino.

Balmerino was not the only example of opposition in Scotland to the Laudian innovations. As early as 1630, Alexander Leighton had been fined £10,000 by Star Chamber for publishing an attack on bishops. Leighton also described Henrietta Maria as a 'daughter of hell'. Alongside the huge fine, Leighton was to have one ear chopped off, his nose slit and his face branded.

A closer look

Early modern punishments

Boring/burning through the tongue

A punishment sometimes used for speaking or writing blasphemously. In a parliamentary debate of the 1650s, it was commented, 'It is an ordinary punishment for swearing, I have known twenty bored through the tongue'.

Branding

Applied with a red-hot iron, branding was to mark the person with their crime. Sometimes a 'B' for blasphemer. In this period, William Prynne was branded with 'SL' for seditious libeller.

Execution

Execution was usually done by hanging or, as in the case of Wentworth and Charles I, by axe. Executions were conducted in public.

Hanging, drawing and quartering

A form of execution for those convicted of treason. The person would be tied to a sledge and pulled through the streets by horses from their prison to the place of execution in London, normally Tyburn or sometimes Charing Cross. At the appointed place, the person was hung until almost dead before being cut down. Brought back to consciousness they were sliced open and their intestines were pulled out and burnt in front of them. The head would be chopped off and the body dismembered, the quartering. The head was normally put on public display, left to rot in a prominent place, while the other parts of the body may have been sent elsewhere for display.

Pillory

A set of stocks in which those to be punished were publicly displayed, pinned by the arms and head, and sometimes abused by onlookers.

Whipping

Sometimes this was done while the person was set in the stocks, tied or, as in the case of John Lilburne on 18 April 1638, it could be as the convicted was dragged through the streets. In Lilburne's case, it has been estimated that as he was dragged from the Fleet Prison to Westminster he would have received nearly 500 lashes.

A closer look

The case of James Nayler, Quaker

One of the consequences of the breakdown of order that accompanied civil war was the growth of religious radicalism and the start of movements that survive until today, like the Quakers. Seen as extremely radical in this period, the Quakers were regarded as a very real threat to society in the 1650s. In 1656, their most prominent leader, James Nayler, entered Bristol on a donkey with his followers laying flowers before him. Nayler was charged with blasphemy for mimicking Christ's entry into Jerusalem. The parliament of the time debated how to punish Nayler. Their debate and the actual punishment meted out on Nayler indicates the nature of 17th-century punishments. There were calls for Nayler to have his tongue slit or bored, to be branded with the letter 'B' for blasphemer. There was even a call by one MP for Nayler to be stoned to death.

Nayler was whipped through the streets of London from the pillory at Westminster to the Old Exchange. In this distance he received 310 lashes. He was then put in the pillory again. Here, his tongue was bored through and his forehead branded with the letter 'B' for blasphemer. Taken to Bristol, the scene of his 'crime', Nayler was put on a horse and ridden into the city facing backwards – this symbolised how he had tried to overturn society's norms. He was then whipped again. Imprisoned, he was expected to undertake hard labour. One of his Quaker followers found that he had no skin left on his back and arms.

Nayler was to die of his wounds in 1660. Nayler, before this date, had probably been the pre-eminent figure in the nascent Quaker movement. With his punishment and subsequent death, the Quaker movement was taken over by his rival George Fox who, at the Restoration, pushed the movement into being more pacifist.

Did you know?

Jenny Geddes

The riot in Edinburgh was sparked by Jenny Geddes throwing her stool at the Dean of St Giles' Cathedral. She proclaimed: 'Deil colic and waame of thee; out, thou false thief. Dost thou say mass at my lug?' In effect, Geddes believed that the prayer book was part of the reintroduction of Catholicism into Scotland.

The key event that was to bring concerted opposition against Charles was his 1633 decision to introduce a new prayer book into Scotland. The fact that it was not ready until early 1637, allowed prearranged nationalist and religious demonstrations to be prepared for its first reading on 23 July 1637. When it was read for the first time in St Giles' Cathedral in Edinburgh, an organised protest became a full-blown riot. The nobility that had organised the protest used this popular support for their cause and maintained control of the opposition to Laudianism.

Fig. 4 *The Arch-Prelate of St Andrews in Scotland reading the new prayer book is assaulted by men and women with cricket bats, stools, sticks and stones*

Another riot in Glasgow at the end of August should have indicated to Charles' councillors in Scotland the seriousness of the opposition. A petition on 20 September signed by a third of the nobility and about 100 clergy indicated the scale of opposition, which was merely confirmed by another riot in Edinburgh on 18 October. Charles' Scottish Privy Council at this point abandoned Edinburgh. In response to this revolt, Charles would not back down and thus pushed moderates to become radicals. A petitioning movement formulated the February 1638 National Covenant.

Fig. 5 *Alexander Henderson*

The National Covenant, principally composed by the Presbyterian radicals Archibald Johnston of Wariston and Alexander Henderson, was a manifesto around which opposition to Charles' religious policy could unite.

Shaped to have the broadest appeal, the National Covenant became the rallying point for a broad Scottish protest movement. Soon, however, a preaching campaign added a radical popular dimension that made the covenanting movement more potentially revolutionary. The covenanters became more radical because of Charles.

> The Covenanters, Charles reasoned, would be defeated because to rebel against one's sovereign was criminal. The rebellion was a simple matter of right or wrong.
>
> 5   Fissel, M., *The Bishops' Wars. Charles I's campaigns against Scotland 1638–1640*, 1994

Charles sent his most trusted Scottish advisor, Hamilton, to Scotland. Hamilton was to negotiate with the covenanters, but only to give Charles time to prepare to crush them.

> I will rather die than yield to these impertinent and damnable demands (as you rightly call them), for it is all one, as to yield to be no King in a very short time.
>
> 6   Charles I addressing Hamilton, June 1638. Taken from Daniels, C. W. and Morrill, J. (eds.), *Charles I*, 1998

> I intend not to yield to the demands of those traitors the Covenanters.
>
> 7   Charles I addressing Hamilton, June 1638. Taken from Daniels, C. W. and Morrill, J. (eds.), *Charles I*, 1998

Activity

Source analysis

1 What do Sources 6 and 7 indicate about Charles' attitude towards the covenanters?

2 Do they support the argument put forward by Fissel in Source 5?

The nature and outcome of the Bishops' Wars

Until 1637 and the Scottish Revolution, there were few visible signs of opposition to Charles' personal rule. The Scottish Revolution exposed problems in England. It was the Scottish Revolution that brought about the crisis of 1637. Charles' determination to crush the Scots resulted in the Bishops' Wars, so-called because of the religious nature of the Scottish opposition to Charles.

> The prayer book rebellion of 1637 was to be the turning point for Charles' government, not only in Scotland, but England and Ireland as well. He had encountered opposition to a number of his policies in all three kingdoms, but this had been containable. The defiance of the Scots changed everything and set in motion a train of events that led to defeat in the Bishops' Wars and, ultimately, the outbreak of civil war.
>
> 8   Cust, R., *Charles I*, 2006

The link between the Scottish Revolution, the Bishops' Wars and the collapse of Charles' personal rule in England is highlighted by the contact between some English peers and the Scottish covenanters. By the summer of 1639, Lord Brooke and Viscount Saye and Sele were in contact with the covenanting leaders. Their shared antipathy to Laudianism made them natural allies. In the 1640s, Saye's son, Nathaniel Fiennes, made a direct parallel between events in 'Britain' and the opposition to the Spanish crown in Catalonia, indicating a grasp of the multiple-kingdom dimension of opposition. The English opponents of Charles understood that if the Scots invaded, Charles would almost certainly need to call an English parliament for finance in which their grievances could be openly voiced and hopefully addressed.

In contrast to the view expressed in Source 13, by 1638, those at the very centre of the regime were more concerned about the future.

> It is not the Scottish business alone that I look upon, but the whole frame of things at home and abroad, with vast expenses out of little treasure, and my misgiving soul is deeply apprehensive of no small evils coming on. God in heaven avert them; but I can see no cure without a miracle, and I fear that will not be showed.

9 *A letter from Laud to Wentworth, 22 June 1638. Taken from Quintrell, B.,* **Charles I 1625–40***, 1993*

Following the outbreak of the Scottish Revolution and Hampden's case, the ship money yield fell dramatically from a 90 per cent collection rate to 20 per cent. Charles tried to deal with the Scots, however, without recourse to parliament, the first monarch to attempt this since 1323.

In order to give himself time to raise an army, Charles had allowed the Scots to call a religious General Assembly at Glasgow. It was clear to the Scots that Charles' concessions were worthless. In November 1638, the assembly proceeded to annul the canons and abolish episcopacy. Charles' army was not ready until April 1639. By then, the Scots were even more prepared to face the King's 15,000 untrained and unruly forces that were assembled. In raising this force, Charles now encountered real problems in getting ship money collected.

> The shortcomings in the royal war effort must also be seen in the context of a general dissatisfaction (or at least unease) in England with many aspects of the Personal Rule. In order to balance the books in the absence of parliamentary subsidies, the king had introduced a range of taxes purely on the basis of his prerogative, in direct challenge to the principle of taxation by consent. Likewise, the Laudian 'new ceremonies' had apparently alienated many people besides the Puritans. Admittedly, opposition to the king's policies had been muted, but this may simply have been because without Parliament it lacked an effective forum. There can be no doubt that domestic resentments, and to a lesser extent pro-Scottish feeling, did indeed retard the king's military preparations.

10 *Scott, D.,* **Politics and War in the three Stuart Kingdoms, 1637–49***, 2004*

 Cross-reference

For more information on the problem of **multiple kingdoms**, see pages 132–3.

 Activity

Thinking point

How useful and reliable is Source 9 as evidence of the viability of Charles' personal rule?

Despite his problems, Charles had an ambitious plan for an attack on Scotland:

- Hamilton would lead an assault by boat on the north-east coast of Scotland with 5,000 men.
- From north Scotland, Lord Huntly would lead a royalist force south and meet Hamilton.
- Both forces would then move further south towards Edinburgh.
- A naval force would blockade the Scottish coasts.
- A naval force would transport a force from Ulster in northern Ireland to west Scotland. This force would be led by the Earl of Antrim, Randall MacDonnell.
- More forces from Ireland would be transported to strengthen the garrison at Carlisle.
- The main English army would assemble near Newcastle and move north.

It was undoubtedly an over-ambitious plan. Facing financial problems and not wanting to recall parliament, Charles negotiated the Truce of Berwick on 18 June 1639 agreeing to a meeting of a Scottish assembly at Edinburgh and parliament, as well as the disbandment of both armies. The covenanters believing that Charles could not be trusted did not disband their army and the Edinburgh assembly and parliament set about reducing royal power in Scotland.

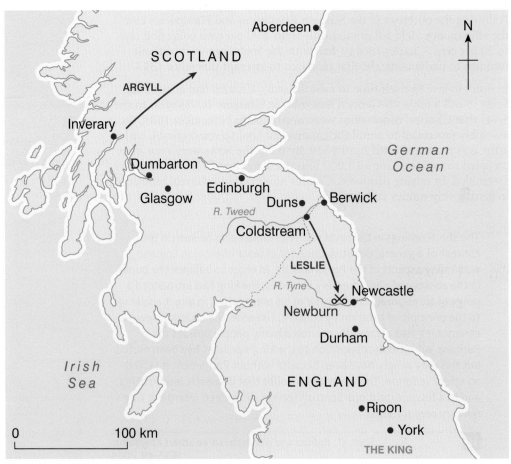

Fig. 6 *The English-Scottish border*

A sign of the scale of the crisis Charles faced is shown by his decision to recall Wentworth from Ireland. On his return in September 1639, Wentworth advised Charles to call an English parliament as the only means of raising money to really fight the Scots.

When this parliament did meet, Charles refused to compromise and dissolved it determined to face the Scots in the field. The Scots did not wait for Charles to send another army to them but crossed the river Tweed and entered England on 20 August 1640 to little resistance.

A closer look

The organisation of covenanting opposition

Source 11, from Scott's book on *Politics and War in the Three Stuart Kingdoms,* deals with the readiness of the covenanting movement to resist Charles I.

The huge increase in Scottish parliamentary and central power under the Covenanters was made possible by their reorganisation of provincial government. A series of gentry-dominated local committees was set up for conscripting, training, and provisioning a national army. For experienced soldiers and arms, the Covenanters looked to the Scottish military and mercantile diaspora in northern Europe. Veterans from the Protestant armies on the Continent flooded home in the late 1630s, and command of the Covenanter forces was given to Alexander Leslie – formerly a senior officer in the Swedish army. In addition, Scottish merchants purchased munitions in Holland and the Baltic and shipped them home with the connivance of sympathetic foreign powers. In order to fund this military expenditure, the local committees oversaw a massive increase in the tax burden. By efficient exploitation of available resources, the Covenanters were able in part to offset Scotland's weakness in men and money relative to England. This in turn is testament to the remarkable power of the Covenant in unleashing human potential at all levels of Scottish society.

11   *Scott, D.,* **Politics and War in the Three Stuart Kingdoms,** **1637–49,** *2004*

Activity

Using bullet points, list all the reasons why the covenanting Scots were well prepared to offer resistance to Charles I.

Key profile

Archibald Campbell, Earl of Argyll, (made Marquess in 1641)

A Presbyterian and head of the Campbell clan, Argyll was therefore a Gaelic Highland chief. The centre of his power was the western Highlands. Part of Argyll's support of the covenanting movement came from the traditional Campbell rivalry with the MacDonald and MacDonnells who were led by the Catholic Earl of Antrim. Charles had considered using Antrim against the covenanters and this had made Argyll more convinced in his stand against the King.

Charles' attempts to raise an army had been poor. There was only a minor encounter between the armies at Newburn but within 10 days the Scots had occupied Newcastle. By the Treaty of Ripon, on 21 October 1640, Charles agreed to pay the Scots £850 a day while they occupied English soil. For this Charles needed another English parliament. This was confirmed for him by the Council of Peers he had assembled at York in September. These Lords would not cooperate with Charles unless he called another parliament. Twelve of the peers, including Bedford and Warwick, produced the Petition of Twelve Peers at the end of August 1640 (see page 104).

Argyll's influence and that of the elite, referred to as a **Oligarchic Centralism**, gave them more control over the covenanter rebellion and thus an advantage in the struggle with Charles I.

Charles' attempts to raise an army had been poor. Alongside continued attempts to collect ship money, Charles called for coat and conduct money. Coat and conduct money was a tax to support the county-trained bands when they had to serve outside their county. It was supposed to provide for food and other expenses like transport. There was widespread opposition to this.

> The repulse at Newburn and the abandonment of Newcastle did not lose the war. Rather, politics had doomed the campaign. The Crown's policies had brought about a major war without parliamentary financial assistance and with a depleted Exchequer. Making war without money had led to these straits. The designs for an amphibious assault on Scotland had forced the Scots' hand and led to a land war for which the English were not prepared. They were unprepared because the King had not harnessed the might of England by establishing first a political consensus through Parliament.

*Fissel, M., **The Bishops' Wars. Charles I's campaigns against Scotland 1638–1640**, 1994*

Another key factor in the Scottish victory and their importance in the early years of the English Civil War was the nature of the two armies. This was also crucial for, according to one historian, Wheeler, Charles' 'failure in the Second Bishops' War was not due to shortages of money'.

■ Key term

Oligarchic Centralism: a term used by the historian Allan Macinnes to describe the prominent role of Scottish nobles in managing the covenanter movement. An oligarchy is government by a small group of persons. Argyll and his fellow noble covenanters managed the parliamentary, policy, military and diplomatic affairs of the covenanting movement. In this way, power and influence was centralised in the hands of a small number of men.

■ Activity

Source analysis

Using Source 12, note down in bullet-point form the reasons for Charles I's defeat in the Bishops' Wars.

■ A closer look

The strength of the covenanter army and weakness of the English

The covenanter army was boosted by the return of many Scots who had been serving as professional soldiers on the continent in the Thirty Years' War. These were battle-hardened troops who knew what they were doing. These troops were used to train those recruited to the cause. Furthermore, although the nobles who raised regiments were given command, it was policy that the positions of lieutenant colonel and sergeant major of every regiment were given to professional soldiers, as were the positions of lieutenant and sergeant at company level. In this way, there was a core directing the army with real expertise.

In comparison, the King used conscripts rather than mobilise the trained bands, the local militia, perhaps because he did not trust their political loyalty. The result was, however, that the army was made up of the 'dregs of society'. As they were marched north, the English army committed robberies, riots and murder.

Was the personal rule viable?

The limited open opposition to Charles' personal rule before 1637 raises the question as to whether his rule would have been viable without the Scottish Revolution.

Fig. 7 *The Scottish Revolution – the end of personal rule?*

In reading the following sources, pay particular attention to evidence of the strengths and weaknesses of the personal rule.

> All things are at this instant here in that calmness that there is very little matter of novelty to write, for there appears no change or alteration either in court or affairs, for all business goes undisturbedly on in the strong current of the present time to which all men for the most part submit, and that effects this quietness. And although payments here are great yet they only privately breathe out a little discontented humour and lay down their purses, for I think that great tax of the ship money is so well digested I suppose it will become perpetual.

13   *John Burghe to Viscount Scudamore, October 1637. Taken from Daniels, C. W. and Morrill, J. (eds.), **Charles I**, 1998*

> By 1637, the monarchy was solvent in terms of income and expenditure, although little had been done to reduce debts. More importantly, a period of prolonged peace had benefited trade, so that revenue from custom duties had risen by more than 50%, promising a possible route to long-term financial security. The situation was still finely balanced, and there is no doubt of the discontent felt by some, but opposition was muted, with little opportunity for open expression. There was clearly some resentment of ship money, of the failure to call Parliament and of the changes in the Church, but little hope of reversing them and the leaders of the Puritan faction were considering emigration as their only way out. Charles appeared to be in control.

14   *Wilkinson, R., **Years of Turmoil. Britain 1603–1714**, 1999*

> By 1637 a combination of political and religious grievances had created opposition among a far wider spectrum of public opinion than the 'Puritan faction'. That opposition, however, had few opportunities to express itself in the absence of a parliament. If Charles could maintain his control of the situation, there was no reason why he could not continue to impose his will. A combination of growing trade and Ship Money offered the prospect of financial independence.

15   *Anderson, A., **Stuart Britain 1603–1714**, 1999*

Activity

Revision exercise

Using Sources 13–15, construct a chart detailing the evidence that suggests that a continuation of the personal rule was viable, and the evidence that suggests that it was not.

Source	Viable	Problems

Learning outcomes

Through your study in this section you should have developed an understanding of examples of opposition to Charles' policies, the nature of opposition in England and the importance of opposition in Scotland in terms of the crisis of 1637.

AQA Examination-style questions

(a) Explain why Charles' religious policies in the years 1633 to 1637 caused concern.   *(12 marks)*

 Examiner's tip

You will need examples of Charles' religious policies. These examples will need to be linked to explanations of why they caused concern. Examples may include the emphasis on outward forms of religion, as well as enforcement through visitations.

You should also think about the dates in the question. What examples are there from 1633 and 1637 or why might these dates be significant?

The key focus in terms of Charles' religious policy is the imposition of Laudianism and why it caused concern. The central reason was the perception of many that there was a drift towards Catholicism. That contemporaries linked Catholicism with absolutism may also be commented on.

(b) Before 1638, the personal rule was a triumph for Charles I.' Explain why you agree or disagree with this view.   *(24 marks)*

 Examiner's tip

An important part of answering such b) part questions will be your introduction. The introduction is designed to indicate your argument clearly and may well indicate the structure of your essay. An introduction has the following key features:

▨ the inclusion of the key words of the questions

▨ some indication of the key themes of the period in question

▨ some indication of a precise example from key content

▨ a clear indication of your argument.

All of this should be done in four to six sentences, expressed clearly and flowing as a coherent paragraph. Introductions are, therefore, hard to do well and you should practise writing them.

With regard to the structure of the rest of your answer, the question could be answered by the following sections:

▨ How Charles' personal rule could be viewed positively.

▨ The problems/discontent Charles' personal rule created.

▨ Assessment.

Each of these sections would then be broken down into paragraphs. For example, in terms of a positive view of Charles' personal rule, this could be split into paragraphs on administration, finance and religion. When considering a more positive view of the personal rule, some reference may be made to Kevin Sharpe.

In considering discontent, some distinction should be made between discontent and open opposition.

Planning of answers is always important.

8   The return of parliament

In this chapter you will learn about:

- the failure of the short parliament

- how the long parliament responded to the crisis

- the development and nature of opposition in the long parliament.

Fig. 1 *Charles I in the House of Lords*

On 15 April 1640, King Charles I made a speech to the assembled parliament that was noted by the MP Sir Thomas Aston in his diary.

> Monarchy Royal is of all sorts of Government, the most excellent. Which in this country I hope none denies, if any do I wish confusion to them.

Within a month, Charles had sent the MPs who listened to him away. Defeated by the Scots in battle, Charles was forced to call another English parliament. This parliament he could not dissolve. This parliament went to war with him in 1642. This parliament legitimised his execution in 1649.

The short parliament

The first English parliament that Charles called in 1640 became known as the short parliament. The short parliament derives its name from the fact that it only lasted from 13 April 1640 until it was dissolved by Charles on 5 May 1640. The historian Derek Hirst has argued that many MPs were returned to parliament in 1640 on an anti-court election platform. Yet, despite a sense of unity about the abuses of the personal rule, there was limited organisation or any real idea of an opposition in modern party political terms. The King could still rely on a majority in the Lords and his announcement of the illegality of ship money won him support in the Commons.

Key chronology

1640 13 April to 5 May	Short parliament.
August	Cumbernauld Band; Second Bishops' War – Treaty of Ripon.
November	Long parliament; Strafford impeached.
December	London Root and Branch Petition; Laud impeached.
1641 February	Triennial Act.
May	Protestation Oath; army plot; death of Bedford.
10 May	Act of Attainder.
12 May	Execution of Wentworth.

It quickly became clear, however, that MPs were not going to vote subsidies for the Scottish war. Key figures in parliament, like Pym and Saye and Sele, were actually in league with the Scots covenanters. Both they and the Scots recognised that a long-term solution to both their problems could only come through concessions to an English parliament by Charles. It is a mark of how far Charles had alienated the English political elite that many MPs were less concerned with their traditional enemy who had an army on their border than their own King. Charles, recognising that only significant concessions would gain him the 12 subsidies he wanted to fight the Scots, dissolved parliament. With parliament dissolved, Charles arrested the three Lords he regarded as his leading critics, Warwick, Brooke, and Saye and Sele. From the Commons, he had Pym and Hampden arrested.

A closer look

English and Scottish relations

In 1603, when the King of Scotland, James VI, also became the King of England as James I the relationship between the two independent kingdoms did change. King James VI and I did immediately announce his desire for a union of the two kingdoms. When this plan was introduced to his first parliament in 1604, however, it encountered bitter opposition from the vast majority of MPs. Not only did they denounce it on constitutional, religious and financial reasons, but they also attacked the Scots as a nation and people. In the union debates of 1604 to 1608, the Scots were portrayed as barbarians. James gave up on any hopes of a union and adopted a gradualist approach. The two kingdoms with one ruler would be brought together slowly over time. Even in 1617, an English description of Scotland by one Weldon stated:

'For the Country I must confess it is too good for those that possess it. The air might be wholesome but for the stinking people that inhabit it. The country, although it be mountainous, affords no monsters but women. To be chained in marriage with one of them were as to be tied to a dead carcass and cast into a stinking ditch.'

Such hatred of the Scots persisted yet, remarkably, the English were willing to allow a Scottish army to occupy northern England – another demonstraion of the alienation Charles engendered.

Charles' approach was to impose uniformity across all his kingdoms, especially in religion. A formal union between England and Scotland was not actually made until, under English pressure, the Scots succumbed in 1707. Ireland became part of the union in 1801. The apparent reversal of this process, the latest part of which has been the establishment of a Welsh assembly and a Scottish parliament, has happened in recent years.

Activity

Thinking point

As a class, debate the advantages and disadvantages from different perspectives of the current relationship between England, Scotland, Wales and Ireland. Divide the class into four groups. Each group should consider the position of one of the four countries.

As part of this, also try to outline what it means to be 'British'. Can 'Britishness' be defined?

Despite the lack of resolution caused by Charles' dissolution of the short parliament, Barry Coward has stated that:

'By 1640 the old constitution was still intact. Nor was it inevitable that it would break down as it did in 1641 and 1642. The causes of this lay largely in events which took place after, not before, 1640.'

Further tension and the development of the crisis that was to end in civil war in England in 1642 was caused by Charles' decision to face the Scots again without parliamentary backing in 1640.

Activity

Thinking point

What does Source 1 say about Charles I's position?

Notwithstanding this dissolution, the King intends vigorously to pursue his former designs, and to levy the same army. About 3 weeks hence, they are to be drawn together, but as yet I can not learn by what means we are certain to get one shilling, towards the defraying [of] this great expense. It grieves my soul to be involved in these counsels; and the sense I have of the miseries that are like to ensue, is held by some a disaffection in me.

 The Earl of Northumberland, Lord General of Charles' army, writing two days after the short parliament was dissolved. Taken from Scarboro, D., England 1625–1660, 2005

Although Charles had dissolved the short parliament, he allowed convocation to continue to sit when normally it would have ended its meeting with the dissolution of parliament. Worse, the convocation passed 17 canons, one of which, the 'et cetera oath' that the Church government would be by 'archbishops, bishops, deans and archdeacons, etc., as it now stands established', for many added to their doubts about Charles' religious intentions. In particular, it aided the radicalisation of the covenanter movement into something more like a popular crusade against the apparent danger of popery in Charles' religious policy.

The Scots crossed the border at the river Tweed on 20 August. They met little resistance and after a minor skirmish at Newburn, the Scots went on to occupy Scotland. The Treaty of Ripon on 21 October 1640 meant that Charles had to pay the Scots £850 a day during their time in England. For this, Charles needed another English parliament. This was confirmed for him by the Council of Peers he had assembled at York in September. These Lords would not cooperate with Charles unless he called another parliament. Twelve of the peers, including Bedford and Warwick, produced the Petition of Twelve Peers at the end of August 1640. In this it was claimed that (Source 2):

> Your Majesty's sacred person is exposed to hazard and danger in the present expedition against the Scottish army, and by occasion of this war your revenue is much wasted, your subjects burdened with coat-and-conduct money, billeting of soldiers, and other military charges, and divers rapines and disorders committed in several parts of this your realm, by the soldiers raised for that service, and your whole kingdom become full of fear and discontents.

 The Petition of Twelve Peers, August 1640

In the Petition the peers also expressed their concerns (Figure 2).

The solution the peers proposed was a calling of parliament.

𝕻𝖊𝖙𝖎𝖙𝖎𝖔𝖓 𝖔𝖋 𝕿𝖜𝖊𝖑𝖛𝖊 𝕻𝖊𝖊𝖗𝖘

- Innovations in religion.
- Increase of popery.
- The bringing in of Irish and foreign forces.
- The attempts to collect ship money.
- The length of time without a parliament.

Fig. 2 *The Petition of Twelve Peers*

■ The long parliament and the development of opposition under John Pym

Defeated in battle and opposed by a majority of the Lords, Charles was forced to call another English parliament, the so-called long parliament, which first sat on 3 November 1640.

Although the majority of MPs wanted change at the start of the long parliament, care is needed with the idea of an 'opposition' to the crown, let alone an organised opposition.

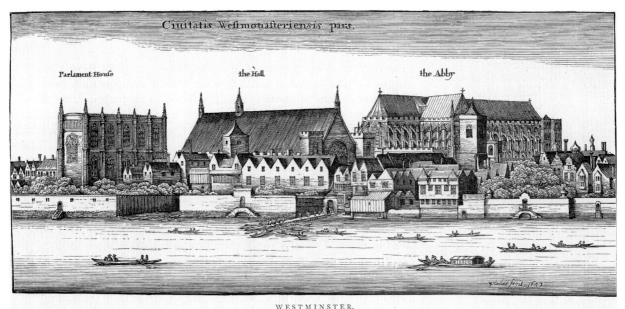

WESTMINSTER.
Temp. Charles I.
After W. Hollar, 1647.

Fig. 3 *Westminster, London*

By the time government collapsed in 1640 there existed a strong desire for widespread change. To do this they had to tear down institutions like the prerogative courts, to transfer to themselves the power of determining the term of their own dissolution, to execute one leading minister and to throw the Archbishop of Canterbury into the Tower.

It was in the Commons that the opposition built its institutional base. During the course of the sixteenth century many things happened to increase Parliament's powers and to diminish the capacity of the Crown to control it. By the early seventeenth century there is the visible beginning of a formal opposition, men who came up to Parliament with a set determination to challenge the Crown on a wide range of issues. Loosely calling themselves 'the Country', they developed their own distinct ideology and tactics.

3   Stone, L., ***The Causes of the English Revolution***, 1972

Stone's work is partly an example of how some Whig and Marxist historians regarded 'opposition'. Of all periods of British History, the causes of the English Civil War has probably provoked more historiography than any other, and there are certainly different ideas about the development and nature of opposition in 1640. Whig and Marxist historians had a similar approach to explaining the causes of the English Civil War in that both saw it as the culmination of long-term causes, some dating it back to the changes in land owning that accompanied the Reformation of the 1530s. For both, there was an element of inevitability about a conflict between crown and parliament as the groups represented by parliament sought to impose their own growing economic and political power at the expense of the monarch. There was an ideological struggle between progressive forces and a backward-looking monarchy. Tension was gradually building up over time until Charles' Eleven Years' Tyranny forced a more concerted

Exploring the detail

Long parliament

This became known as the long parliament in comparison to the brevity of the previous parliament. In December 1648, some MPs were purged from the parliament to leave what became known as the rump parliament, which authorised the trial and execution of Charles I. This rump parliament was ended by Cromwell in 1653 but returned under his son, Richard, in 1659 and the purged members of 1648 were allowed back into parliament in February 1660, prompting the return of monarchy.

Activity

Source analysis

What arguments are put forward in Source 3 about the nature of opposition in 1640?

■ Exploring the detail

The Triennial Act

The Triennial Act stipulated that Charles had to call a parliament every three years and that it should last a minimum of 50 days. If the King failed to do this, the writs for calling parliament would be done automatically by the Lord Chancellor. The act therefore ensured that there could not be another period of prolonged personal rule.

opposition. For both Whigs and Marxists, then, there was a clearly defined 'opposition' to the crown that seized its moment in the long parliament.

More recent interpretations would suggest that, in 1640, the majority of the Commons was united not in the sense of an opposition party but more in general terms against the abuses of the personal rule. This general unity was illustrated by the incarceration of Wentworth and Laud in the Tower of London, the abolition of the Courts of Star Chamber and High Commission, ship money, tonnage and poundage and the passage of the Triennial Act on 15 February 1641.

In contrast to Whig or Marxist interpretations, revisionist historians regarded the unity that passed such measures as the Triennial Act as resonant of the general consensus among the English political elite, rather than there being an organised opposition grouping. Civil war in England was due to short-term causes, particularly from the outbreak of the Scottish Revolution of 1637, but predominantly events in late 1641.

Post-revisionism sees different political ideas underlying the general consensus. Some regarded resistance to a monarch who aimed at absolutism as legitimate in light of ideas that they were bound by their oath to the law.

The short parliament – 13 April to 5 May 1640

> At least two markedly different constitutional theories were voiced throughout the period. Of course, some men were confused, or apathetic, or ill-informed on constitutional questions. Others attempted to tone down their claims for the sake of preserving harmony. Nevertheless differences of constitutional principle contributed to political conflict, especially when they were applied to issues involving property or taxation. It was in connection with such issues that the King or his ministers were usually accused of attempting to introduce arbitrary government. Many Englishmen argued that the King's powers were derived from the people or from the laws of the realm, and that the King did not have to be obeyed if his orders conflicted with law.

4   *Sommerville, J., **Ideology, property and the constitution**, 1989*

The long parliament – 1640 to 1660

Fig. 4 *The short and long parliaments*

Like the revisionists, however, post-revisionists do not believe these different ideas were a real political issue until practical problems brought them to the surface after 1637. In some ways, post-revisionist interpretations have led to the re-emergence in historical accounts of the idea of an opposition group in parliament.

 Activity

Revision exercise

Using the information in this chapter so far, construct a chart showing a summary of the main points of the interpretations of Whigs, Marxists, revisionists and post-revisionists in relation to opposition.

Once you have listed what you think are the main points of each interpretation, you may wish to reorder the material to illustrate how the interpretations agree and differ.

Whig	Marxist	Revisionist	Post-revisionist

Men like Warwick, Bedford, Saye and Sele and Pym clearly had a religious and political perspective different from the King's that could see them termed as an opposition group, although it should also be noted that there were differences in their approach. In general terms, the group around the Earl of Warwick was more aggressive in their opposition than the group around the Earl of Bedford, who was much more inclined to keep negotiation with the King as open as possible.

Edward Hyde isolated the individuals shown in Table 1 as the 'governing party', the leading opposition figures in the Lords and Commons in the long parliament.

Table 1

Lords	Commons
Robert Devereux, 3rd Earl of Essex	Nathaniel Fiennes
William Fiennes, Viscount Saye and Sele	John Hampden
Robert Greville, 2nd Lord Brooke	Denzil Holles
Edward Montagu, Viscount Mandeville	John Pym
Francis Russell, 4th Earl of Bedford	Oliver St John
Robert Rich, 2nd Earl of Warwick	William Strode
Philip, 4th Lord Wharton	Sir Henry Vane Jnr

Despite different ideas about religion and politics, no one wanted a civil war. The continued attempt at settlement can be seen most clearly in the Earl of Bedford's scheme to reform Charles' rule from within through 'bridge appointments'.

 Did you know?

In 1641, the Earl of Warwick and the Bishop of Lincoln nearly had a fight in the House of Lords. Warwick thought that the bishop had mocked him by referring to him by the derogatory term 'sirrah' (lowly) rather than 'sir'.

■ **Key profile**

Francis Russell, 4th Earl of Bedford

The Earl of Bedford (1587–1641) was a leading opposition figure. Bedford aimed to enter Charles' government with others like Pym to guarantee 'good government'. Bedford took a key role in the proposed financial settlement, which would mean that Charles would not need to exploit his prerogative. On 19 February 1641, he was appointed, along with six others, including Saye, Essex and Mandeville, as one of Charles' councillors. Oliver St John became Solicitor-General. From this point, the fact that the meetings of the council became much less frequent indicates Charles' reluctance to really settle with Bedford. What really undermined Bedford's scheme was the Scots. In a paper of 24 February 1641, they demanded the abolition of bishops and Wentworth's death, both of which Bedford needed to sideline to get agreement from Charles. Without the Scots, however, Bedford and his allies would be exposed to Charles' vengeance. While he seems willing to have risked pushing ahead with settlement, others, like Warwick, also wanted Wentworth dead. By mid-March there was no hope of Bedford's scheme working. On 10 May 1641, Bedford died of smallpox.

Fig. 5 *Francis Russell, 4th Earl of Bedford*

With Charles' 'evil counsellors', Wentworth and Laud, imprisoned and facing trial, Bedford and his allies, notably John Pym in the Commons, sought Charles' agreement to abolishing the most confrontational financial and political aspects of the personal rule, as well as a return to an Elizabethan-based broad Protestant Church. To ensure this, Bedford would enter government as Lord Treasurer with Pym as Chancellor of the Exchequer. Charles would receive a financial settlement, although one that tied him to parliament. Therefore, a solution would be arrived at without a fundamental change to the system, just a change to the management of the political system. Conrad Russell has argued that Bedford's settlement plans 'were not an opposition programme, but an attempt, with backing from inside the heart of government, to drag the King kicking and screaming into the real world, and thereby to reunite the country'. On 19 February 1641, some progress appeared to have been made when Bedford, along with Saye, Mandeville and Essex were appointed by Charles to his Privy Council, although the meetings of that body then became much less frequent.

Part of the negotiation of these 'bridge appointments' seems to have revolved around Charles' desire for Wentworth not to be executed. Bedford, and perhaps even Pym according to some historians, therefore may have tried to moderate the proceedings against Wentworth so that, while he would be punished, he would not be executed. Others, like Warwick, were determined that Wentworth should be executed. The issue of what to do with Wentworth could be seen as prompting a more opposition-minded response in parliament, at least initially.

Wentworth had been recalled from Ireland in 1639 to aid Charles in facing the Scots. He was regarded by many in parliament as the man with the potential to make Charles absolutist. The focus on Wentworth was due to the danger he appeared to represent and the fact that he was used as a scapegoat. It was safer to blame 'evil counsellors', men like Wentworth and Laud, for the crisis than Charles. Firstly, there was the very real risk of punishment for openly criticising the King. Secondly, if it was openly admitted that Charles was the root cause of the problems they faced, MPs would be questioning the whole system that governed everyone's day-to-day life. For the monarch was God's representative on earth and the pinnacle of a system that tied the whole population together, what contemporaries referred to as 'the great chain of being'. A direct attack on Charles risked undermining this system and perhaps prompting demands from those lower in the order of society for change. Without his 'evil counsellors', Wentworth and Laud, it was hoped that Charles would clearly see the need to accept reform and rule with parliament. Furthermore, rather than change the whole system, the removal of counsellors like Wentworth and Laud would also see their replacement with men like Bedford and Pym who would ensure good government.

> Condemnation of Strafford, in particular, became synonymous with the pursuit of justice. Strafford had become the emblem (and in many ways the explanation) of the Personal Rule: kill Strafford, and the Personal Rule died with him. The value of simplistic conspiracy theories of the sort that attached to Strafford was that they could explain political malpractice and conflict without impugning the basic political structure of the realm, and without doing any damage to the fundamental conviction that, left to itself, the political system naturally worked towards unity and consensus, and was not in need of any radical surgery.

5   *Kilburn and Milton, A., 'The public context of the trial and execution of Strafford'*

The removal of Wentworth actually became more about what he might do rather than what he had done. Much of the fear of what Wentworth might do was centred on a concern at what use might be made of forces in Ireland or the King's army in the north of England. Could Wentworth make use of these to destroy the Scots and then turn on the English opposition? Wentworth was impeached in November 1640 at the very beginning of the long parliament. Wentworth's trial before parliament did not start until March 1641.

John Pym was one of the leading figures in prosecuting the impeachment charge against Wentworth.

> The Earl of Strafford has endeavoured by his words, actions and counsels to subvert the fundamental law of England and Ireland and to introduce an arbitrary and tyrannical government.
>
> Law entitles a king to the allegiance and service of his people; it entitles the people to the protection and justice of the king. The law is the boundary between the king's prerogative and the people's liberty. But if the prerogative of the king overwhelms the liberty of the people it will be turned into tyranny, if liberty undermines the perogative, it will grow into anarchy.
>
> It cannot be for the honour of the king that his sacred authority should be used in the practice of injustice and oppression, that his name should be applied to patronize such horrid crimes as have been represented in evidence against the Earl of Strafford.

6   *John Pym's reply to Strafford's defence, 13 April 1641*

Activity

Thinking point

As a class, discuss the following questions:

1. Avoiding suggesting that there was a problem with the system of government was so important for many of the political nation. Explain why.

2. Why was Wentworth, the Earl of Strafford, picked as an 'emblem' by the parliamentary opposition for Charles I's personal rule?

Fig. 6 *John Pym*

Activity

Thinking point

Using bullet points and your own words, summarise Pym's argument based on Source 6.

Very skilfully, Wentworth defended himself. He was well aware of the limited actual evidence against him.

■ Activity

Thinking point

Using bullet points and your own words, summarise Strafford's argument based on Source 7.

Here I am charged to have designed the overthrow both of religion and the state. The first seems to have been used rather for making me odious than guilty. Never a servant in authority beneath the king my master was more hated and maligned, and am still, by the popish faction, than myself, and that for a strict and impartial execution of the laws against them. Hence your Lordships may observe that the greater number of witnesses used against me, whether my grey hairs to be charged with the mistakes of the times. [My accusers] tell me that they speak in defence of the commonweal against my arbitrary laws; give me leave to say that I speak in defence of the commonweal against their arbitrary treason.

7 *The Earl of Strafford's last speech in his defence, 13 April 1641*

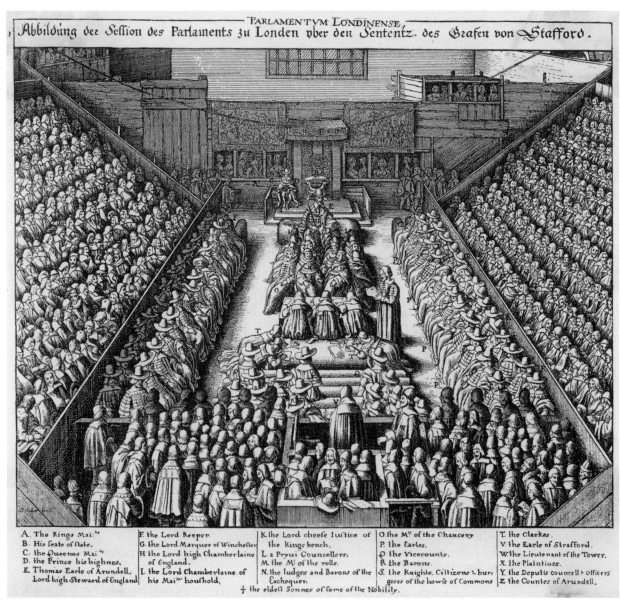

A. The Kings Mai.ᵗⁱᵉ
B. His feate of ftate.
C. the Queenes Mai.ᵗⁱᵉ
D. the Prince his highnes.
E. Thomas Earle of Arundell, Lord high Steward of England
F. the Lord Keeper.
G. the Lord Marques of Winchefter
H. the Lord high Chamberlaine of England.
I. the Lord Chamberlaine of his Maiᵗⁱᵉˢ houfhold,
K. the Lord cheefe Iuftice of the Kings bench.
L. 2 Pryui Councellors.
M. the Mˡ of the rolls.
N. the Iudges and Barons of the Exchequer.
O. the Mˡ of the Chancery
P. the Earles.
Q. the Vicecounts.
R. the Barons.
S. the Knights, Cittizens & bur gefes of the howfe of Commons
T. the Clarkes.
V. the Earle of Strafford.
W. the Lieutenant of the Tower.
X. the Plaintiues.
Y. the Deputis councell & officers
Z. the Countes of Arundell.
† the eldeft Sonnes of fome of the Nobility.

Fig. 7 *The trial of Thomas Wentworth*

The evidence against Wentworth was essentially circumstantial. The key charge, that he designed to bring an Irish army for Charles to control England, centred on one witness, Sir Henry Vane senior. Vane, in his role as secretary, had been present at a meeting in May 1640 of the Privy Council's Council of War. His son, Sir Henry Vane junior, had a copy of his father's notes. The key part of these notes was Wentworth's comment to Charles:

> You have an army in Ireland, you may imploy here to reduce this kingdome.

The issue with this statement was what Wentworth meant by 'here' and 'this kingdome'. In the context of the meeting, the most likely reading is a reference to Scotland but those who wanted the execution of Wentworth wanted 'kingdome' read as England.

With the limits of the evidence and Wentworth's adept defence of himself it appeared as if he might escape execution. Many in parliament were fed up with the time spent on a prosecution that appeared to be going nowhere. It was therefore decided to proceed against Wentworth by means of a Bill of Attainder. This medieval method allowed anyone who was seen as a threat to the State to be removed by parliament without the need of a formal trial. While some, like Warwick, wanted this pursued vigorously, others, like Bedford, seem to have been more cautious. Bedford was still negotiating appointment to Charles' government and, in return, was trying to ensure that Wentworth's punishment did not extend to execution. The limits to Bedford's influence became clear however when, on 24 February 1641, the Scots made clear that they would not stand for anything less than the end of bishops and the death of Wentworth. According to one of the leading covenanters, Johnston of Wariston, when Charles read of the Scots' views on bishops and Wentworth he went 'starke mad'.

At this point, however, the actions of Charles I, not for the first time, heightened the political tension and undermined Wentworth's position. On 19 April, it became known that Charles had just ordered all officers to return to their commands with the English army in the north. This was interpreted as a plan to organise the army and use it against parliament, which rumours had it he was intending to dissolve. It was the revelation of the army plot that also spurred the Commons to pass the Bill of Attainder, 204 votes to 59.

On one level, this vote would indicate a substantial majority in favour of executing Wentworth. It should be noted however that the total votes cast represent about only half of the total MPs. Many simply did not vote or absented themselves from the House. Increasingly, when it came to making real decisions only the more committed were prepared to act. John Pym was chosen to carry the Attainder Bill to the Lords for their consideration. When Pym got to the Lords, Saye and Sele, one of his erstwhile political allies, had claimed illness and gone home to bed. A very sparsely attended House of Lords eventually assented to the Attainder Bill.

On 3 May, more concrete rumours of an 'army plot' were revealed by Pym to parliament.

The army plot saw parliament pass a bill that meant that they could not be dissolved without their own consent, which Charles agreed to on 10 May. They also drew up the Protestation Oath. The Oath was designed to bind MPs together in this apparent time of crisis. The language of

Activity

Source analysis

How far does Source 7 differ from Source 6 in relation to the attitudes to the exercise of political authority by Wentworth, the Earl of Strafford?

Exploring the detail

Army plot

The plot centred around an attempt by a group of officers to seize the Tower of London, release Wentworth and dissolve parliament. The evidence for Charles' involvement was circumstantial but, given his track record since 1625, it was easy for many MPs to believe he had some role in the plot. This first army plot was followed by a second after Wentworth's execution, which essentially again revolved around military force against parliament. Tellingly, Pym did not reveal the second plot until October 1641 when he felt it would be more to his advantage.

Activity

Thinking point

Discuss the following:

1 In what ways was parliament a 'representative of the people' in 1640?

2 In what ways was parliament not a 'representative of the people' in 1640?

3 In what ways is parliament a 'representative of the people' today?

the Oath is indicative of the tension at Westminster. In the preamble to the Protestation Oath there was reference to 'endeavours to subvert the fundamental laws of England and Ireland, and to introduce the exercise of an arbitrary and tyrannical government by most pernicious and wicked counsels, practices, plots and conspiracies'. To counter this threat of absolutism, MPs were expected to swear the Oath to defend the privileges of parliament but, perhaps more telling, swear their allegiance to 'the true reformed Protestant religion' against 'all popery and popish innovation'. Once more, the Protestation Oath indicates the contemporary belief that Catholicism and absolutism went hand in hand.

> The Protestation sought in practical terms to underline Parliament's role as the representative of the people.

8   Hughes, A., *The Causes of the English Civil War*, 1998

Fig. 8 *Old London Bridge and Traitors' gate*

The Protestation Oath prompted people into action, for those who agreed with it were expected to subscribe to it. In a London parish, when the community gathered to consider the Protestation Oath in their church, John Blackwell addressed them:

> Gentlemen, we have here made a Protestation before almighty God against all popery and popish innovations, and these rails (laying his hand upon the rails about the communion table) are popish innovations, and therefore it is fit they be pulled down, and shall be pulled down.

To become an act, the Attainder Bill and therefore Wentworth's execution needed the royal assent. It was in the heightened atmosphere of the army plot and Protestation Oath with the presence of the London crowd increasingly felt, that Charles, fearing for his family, especially his Catholic wife, gave his assent and thus condemned Wentworth to death.

Cross-reference

For details of the **Root and Branch Petition**, see page 120.

A closer look

The London crowd or mob

This was a negative term given to the population of London who participated in politics. This participation happened at different levels. At its lowest level, as the term denotes, it was a derogatory term based on fear of popular revolution. Other accounts indicate how the more prosperous members of London society also turned out to support parliament. Politicians at Westminster were well aware of the potential of mobilising support in London for their campaigns. The role of London can be seen in the 15,000 who signed the Root and Branch Petition, as well as Pym's desire to publish the Grand Remonstrance just as Charles I returned from Scotland in November 1641. The London crowd also came out to defend the Tower of London in early May 1641 amid rumours of a royalist plot to seize it and release Wentworth. London was, however, a sophisticated and complex political arena with its own centuries-established, multi-layered systems of government and representation. One such was the Common Council. The elections for this body in December 1641 produced a much more radical body who were more willing to organise popular support for Pym. Over Christmas 1641, the London crowd was used to put pressure on the Lords to exclude bishops. When, in February 1642, the King agreed to their exclusion, the Commons asked London ministers to control crowds that then disappeared, indicating the influence of the Puritan network.

The London population was an acutely aware political audience and the use of the London crowd was part of the strategy of the parliamentary leaders.

> Religious networks and colonial interests gave any members of both Houses contacts with the city. London Puritan merchants who were involved in the North American colonial trades had particularly close contacts with independents, artisans and ordinary city consumers. Such men played a major part in channelling popular demonstrations, but this is not to say that they manipulated or distorted popular opinion. Support for Parliament, and fear of evil counsellors and popish conspiracy were clearly widespread in the City in 1640–42.
>
> **9**   Hughes, A., *The Causes of the English Civil War*, 1998

The use of the London population and their willingness to support the parliamentary cause also, however, benefited Charles.

> While the use of the mob and the practice of tumultuary petitioning were undoubtedly used ruthlessly by Pym and his radical City allies, it is more than likely that the atmosphere created by such happenings did more to win support for the king than his opponents. Royalist propaganda was certainly to make the most of the opportunities presented by these incidents.
>
> **10**   Ashton, R., *The City and the Court 1603–1643*, 1979

Fig. 9 *Selling printed ballads in the street in 17th-century London*

As the country divided, so too did London.

> Civil war became inevitable when City and parliamentary conflicts became fully merged through the consolidation of alliances between the City radical movement and the opposition in Parliament, on the one hand, and the City conservative movement and the Crown, on the other. Representatives of the merchant elite were, of course, at the core of proroyal forces in London from the return of Parliament in 1640. But a City royalist movement was fully consolidated only from the second half of 1641. It came to include both longtime supporters of the court and former backers of antiabsolutist reform who chose to ally with the Crown in order to oppose the increasingly radical aspirations of a London popular movement led by nonmerchant citizens and tied ever more closely to the opposition in Parliament.

11   *Brenner, R.,* **Merchants and Revolution. Commerical Change, Political Conflict, and London's Overseas Traders, 1550–1653,** *1993*

As Wentworth's fate became clearer, Charles wrote to him:

> The misfortune that is fallen upon you by the strange mistaking and conjuncture of these times, being such that I must lay by the thought of employing you hereafter in my affairs; yet I cannot satisfy myself in honour or conscience without assuring you (now in the midst of your troubles), that upon the word of a king you shall not suffer in life, honour, or fortune. This is but justice, and therefore a very mean reward from a master to so faithful and able a servant as you have showed yourself to be; yet it is as much as I conceive the present times will permit, though none shall hinder me from being your constant, faithful friend.

12   *Charles I to Strafford, 23 April 1641*

Activity

Source analysis

Using Source 12, note down the message Wentworth would have got from Charles' letter.

The impact of the crowd clearly made Charles consider his and his family's safety.

Fig. 10 *Charles I and his wife Henrietta Maria of France*

Wentworth increasingly appeared to be a necessary scapegoat, a sacrifice to achieve settlement or prevent a direct attack on monarchy.

As a last resort, Charles appealed to the House of Lords for mercy.

> I did yesterday satisfy the justice of the kingdom, by the passing of the Bill of Attainder against the Earl of Strafford; but mercy being as inherent and inseparable to a king as justice, I desire, at this time, in some measure, to show that likewise, by suffering that unfortunate man to fulfil the natural course of his life in a close imprisonment.
>
> But, if no less than his life can satisfy my people, I must assent.
>
> If he must die, it were a charity to reprieve him until Saturday.
>
> Your unalterable and affectionate friend.

13 *Charles asks Lords for mercy, 11 May 1641*

When Wentworth heard he was to be sacrificed he commented, from Psalm 146.3: 'Put not your trust in princes.' Wentworth was executed on 12 May in front of a crowd of about 100,000. Having had to consent to Wentworth's execution, Charles is said to have been less inclined to attempt a negotiated solution. The execution of Wentworth and, more fundamentally, the death of Bedford from illness on 10 May 1641 were, quite literally, the death knell for the 'bridge-appointment' scheme that may have yielded a settlement to the political crisis of 1641. Charles was now less inclined to compromise and Bedford who may have acted as a link between monarch and parliament was removed.

Some historians have regarded the events of 1641 as a 'revolution'.

> The year 1641 saw crisis compound into revolution. The King let his prerogative unravel, submitting to triennial and semi-permanent parliaments, permitting the execution of the Earl of Strafford, and allowing the abolition of such powerful prerogative instruments as the courts of Star Chamber and High Commission. Episcopal authority crumbled, ecclesiastical discipline ceased to operate, and a variety of radical ideas clamoured for attention.

14 *Cressy, D., **England on Edge. Crisis and Revolution 1640–1642**, 2006*

With Bedford's death, those who attempted other ways to a solution through parliament, notably Pym, actually created more division and, in doing so, allowed a royalist party to form. Without this division in parliament there would not have been civil war in England in 1642, as there would not have been two sides to fight a civil war. In explaining why there was a civil war in England, then, it is vital to explain the division of parliament and the formation of a royalist party.

A closer look

The idea of 'revolution'

It is clear that no matter what terms are used for this period of crisis from 1637 through to the eventual restoration of monarchy in 1660, whether 'revolution', 'rebellion' or 'revolt', and whatever period of these 13 years different historians regard as 'revolutionary' the upheaval had an impact for future revolutionaries in America in

 Activity

Source analysis

What do Sources 12 and 13 indicate about Charles' attitude to the proceedings against Wentworth?

the 1770s, for France in the 1780s and Russia after the First World War. Christopher Hill, the great Marxist historian of the English Revolution, naturally stressed this. He wrote:

'Historians often comment on the fact the English Revolution had no ideological forebears. None of the participants knew that what they were living through was a revolution. The word was to acquire its modern meaning only in and because of the English Revolution, the first great European revolution. American revolutionaries consciously looked back to 17th-century English experience.

Englishmen had to face totally unexpected revolutionary situations in the 1640s and 1650s with no theoretical guidance and no experience of any previous event that had been called a revolution. They had to improvise. The Bible in English was the book to which they naturally turned for guidance. It was God's Word, whose authority no one could reject. And it was central to the inheritance of the protestant English nation.'

Summary questions

1 Explain the nature of the opposition to Charles in the long parliament.

2 Explain how worried Charles should have been by the events outlined in this chapter.

9 Parliamentary radicalism and constitutional royalism

Fig. 1 *Charles I demanding the surrender of the five MPs. The Speaker, William Lenthall, kneels before the King saying he has seen nothing of the men*

At the start of January 1642, Charles I marched into the Commons accompanied by several hundred loyal soldiers. His aim was to arrest five MPs and in a stroke remove parliamentary opposition to his rule. When he arrived, he found that the MPs in the foreknowledge of his arrival had already left. Humiliated, Charles had merely united opinion in parliament and London against him. Of the five men Charles aimed to remove from parliament, one particularly stood out, John Pym.

Activity

Using the information in this chapter on John Pym, construct a chart listing 'his tactics', the methods by which he tried to address his chief aim: a religious and political settlement that Charles could not overturn.

Tactics/ method	Problem to address
Chairman of Recess Committee	Ensure parliament continued to focus on settlement despite recess
'Bridge appointments'	Ensuring 'good government'

Cross-reference

For more information on the **politics of Ireland** during this period, see pages 63–66.

John Pym, his aims and tactics

John Pym emerged as the leading figure in the House of Commons in the long parliament and was regarded as a chief opponent of Charles I. His main aims were interlinked and can be seen as:

- the removal and punishment of Charles I's 'evil counsellors'
- a political settlement without the threat of being overturned by Charles I
- the removal of the threat of popery and the establishment of a strong Protestantism.

What linked these three for Pym was what Professor John Morrill has called his 'obsession' with 'true religion'. In establishing the 'true religion', the threat of popery and other threats to it would be removed. The political settlement could not be isolated from the religious settlement. Charles' policies in the 1630s were interpreted as a dual policy of establishing Catholicism and absolutism. Removing the abuses of the personal rule would strength England politically and lessen the threat of popery and absolutism. Restoring a truly Protestant Church for Pym would also strengthen England politically.

> I see no reason to doubt that men like John Pym were genuinely convinced both of the reality of the popish plot and of the need to take up arms to defend the nation from it. In their account of the plot, the radicals around Pym saw Charles as a man whose mind had been so poisoned by the lies and deceptions of the papists that he was no longer capable of defending his office or the realm.

1   *Morrill, J., The Nature of the English Revolution, 1993*

Initially, Pym's agenda was not radical. He himself was, in many ways, not radical. In the 1620s he had sought the adequate funding of royal government and wanted the political nation unified. Rather than an opponent, Pym could be seen as someone who wanted Charles' government reformed. Pym became more radical during the long parliament as Charles continued to threaten to use force, as a result of the heightened religious and political tension created by the Irish Rebellion.

To achieve his aims, Pym's chief methods were:

- the impeachment of Wentworth and Laud
- a working alliance with the covenanters as military protection for parliament
- Bedford's 'bridge appointments' scheme
- use of parliamentary finance to control Charles
- use of parliamentary committees to steer parliament towards settlement
- parliament to transfer to itself some of the key prerogative powers of the crown.

John Pym

Pym (1583–1643) was from minor gentry. In 1624, he became MP for Tavistock through the influence of the Earl of Bedford but he also had the Earl of Warwick as a patron. Another link to Warwick was through Pym's treasurership of the Providence Island Company, which also tied him to Saye, Brooke, Mandeville and St John. In the parliament of 1625, Pym attacked Montagu, regarding Arminians as papists. In the parliament of 1626, he was involved in the attempted impeachment of Buckingham alongside Bedford and Warwick. The forced loan of 1626 was paid by his brother-in-law at which Pym wrote to the receiver 'though I conceive my brother Hooke payd this mony out of his desire of my safety, yet I fynde my self very hartely greved that he should write that I had sent it'. In the parliament of 1628, Pym launched an attack on Mainwaring who had preached in defence of the forced loan. Pym also played a key role in the passage of the Petition of Right.

While Pym was highly visible in the parliaments of the 1620s, he was pre-eminent in the Commons of 1640 to 1642, to the extent that from the autumn of 1641 he was referred to as 'King Pym'. The latest study of Pym by Conrad Russell argued that Pym was 'not a particularly good politician'. Pym was 'destitute of humour' and 'lacked the politician's crucial ability to read the mood of the house'. The great Victorian historian of the Civil War, Gardiner, argued that Pym 'worked by influence not by eloquence'. Pym emerged in 1640 because most of the other leading MPs of the 1620s were dead. More importantly, the crisis mood of 1640–2 fitted exactly with Pym's strengths. Russell has argued that what 'made Pym a successful parliamentary politician was his total inner certainty, and the emotional force this gave to his performances'.

Pym was involved in Bedford's 'bridge appointments' scheme as a potential Chancellor of the Exchequer. As part of this scheme, he opposed the shift from impeachment to attainder for Wentworth. What pushed Pym to become more radical was Charles I. Crucial in this was the army plot. Russell has argued that 'it was the revelation of the King's readiness to fight rather than settle which finally made Pym irreconcilable. There is no evidence of serious negotiation between Pym and the King after this date'. By June 1641, in the Ten Propositions, Pym wanted the lord lieutenants and their deputies selected by parliament. Even for some of his political allies this was going too far and the proposal can be seen as the forerunner of the Militia Ordinance. Pym constructed a standing committee for parliament to remain vigilant even during the recess of 8 September to 20 October 1641. Pym also strengthened his political influence by making use of the London crowd. The passing of the Grand Remonstrance was timed to come immediately before the King's belated return from Scotland on 25 November 1641. In January 1642, at the time of the Five Members' Coup when Pym was selected for arrest by Charles as one of his leading opponents, the newly-elected more radical London Common Council essentially gave Pym the control of the capital, which the King fled in fear for the safety of his family. There could be no direct attack on Charles but the King's actions in trying to seize the arsenal at Hull and then raising his standard at Nottingham meant that he had declared war.

Cross-reference

For more information on the:

- **army plot**, see page 111
- **Ten Propositions**, see page 123
- **Militia Ordinance**, see page 130
- **Five Members' Coup**, see page 128.

What drove Pym most was his Puritanism. This provided, in the words of the historian Hexter, one of Pym's biographers, 'the emotional basis of his policies'. What motivated Pym was his Puritan hatred of Catholicism. Pym even made a proposal that Catholics should be forced to wear a distinctive mark of dress. Pym was largely responsible for the Commons order of 8 September ordering the destruction of altars, rails and crucifixes and other monuments of superstition. Pym's Puritanism was why he, and others, became more radical as a result of the Irish Rebellion and its political consequences.

> A true revolution needs ideas to fuel it. Puritanism provided an essential element in the Revolution. Without the ideas, the organisation and the leadership supplied by Puritanism, there would be no revolution at all.

2 *Adapted from Stone, L.,* ***The Causes of the English Revolution,*** *1972*

> Puritanism for Charles I was the disease. The royal fear of Puritanism was at its heart a dread of disorder, disunity, and the contamination of 'popularity'. In fact the attempt to eradicate these cancers constituted the salient marks of much royal policy throughout the reign. The king's insecurity, isolation, intransigence, and inability to understand others meant that he easily succumbed to theories of Puritan-inspired conspiracies. Prerogative rule and the reconstruction of the Church after 1629 constituted the royal response to a sincerely held conviction that there existed a deeply entrenched plot, orchestrated by popular Puritan elements in the Commons and within the judiciary, to undermine monarchy.

3 *Davies, J.,* ***The Caroline Captivity of the Church: Charles I and the Remoulding of Anglicanism, 1625–1641,*** *1992*

Activity

Source analysis

According to Source 3, how would Charles have viewed Pym?

Puritanism was the force behind the Root and Branch Petition drawn up by 15,000 Londoners in December 1640 demanding the end of episcopacy, bishops in the Church. One of the criticisms of the bishops in the petition was that they maintained that 'the Pope is not anti-christ'. When this petition was debated in February 1641 it caused division. Pym has traditionally been seen as one of the chief supporters of the Root and Branch Petition. Yet Pym did not aim at the destruction of the Church. He sought the removal of Charles' influence by establishing a system of lay patronage in place of the bishops. This would mean that local communities would be more in control of their church, the vicar and the type of service. As the Arminians were very much a minority supported by the King, this would enable the Church to revert back, in most cases, to moderate Protestantism. Probably the most important of Pym's aims was the preservation of a strongly Protestant Church of England.

Many saw the dismantling of the structure of the Church of England, especially the removal of bishops, as undermining the whole order of society in the manner of James I's statement at the Hampton Court Conference of 1604, 'no bishop, no king'. Men such as Hyde, Colepeper, Falkland and Digby who were in essence moderate Protestants all became supporters of Charles I as the symbol of the Church and order. The historian Smith has argued 'no other debate so accurately prefigured subsequently political allegiance at so early a date'.

There was clearly disagreement on what to replace Laudianism with. While Laud was impeached he was not executed until 1645 and a similar lack of resolution to the issue of the Root and Branch Petition was in part prompted by a need to avoid contentious issues. Religion was the most contentious issue. Petitions arrived for MPs from across the country in support of Root and Branch reform, as well as others in support of bishops as a reaction for order. These indicate the potential for religious division across the country.

All that the Commons could agree on was that the secular powers of bishops should be curtailed and an Exclusion Bill, that they should no longer sit and vote in the House of Lords. This was sent to the Lords in March 1641, but rejected on 8 June 1641. In the Grand Remonstrance of November 1641, it was announced that an Assembly of Divines, in effect a parliament of church men, was to be held at Westminster to discuss religious settlement. In this manner, Pym and his allies made sure further discussion of religious settlement that might provoke more division was sidelined. The Westminster Assembly of Divines did not meet until July 1643. Although an ardent Protestant, Pym was politically pragmatic enough to see the dangers posed by division over religion. With the issue sidelined, focus could be on achieving a political settlement.

Cross-reference

For more information on the **Grand Remonstrance**, see page 126.

Pym's importance

Pym, as one of the foremost critics of Charles I, had a role in most of the key political issues of 1640 to 1642. He worked with the covenanters, realising that the initial survival of the long parliament depended on their army of occupation in the north of England, no matter how unpopular it increasingly became. He was at the forefront of stressing the dangers of the army plot and the general popish plot. He took a leading role in attacking Wentworth and supported the Protestation Oath. In November 1641, he was to be a key figure behind the introduction of the Grand Remonstrance (see page 106).

Pym's prominence is illustrated by the labels, often derogatory, '**King Pym**' or of '**Pym's Junto**'.

Key terms

King Pym: this term was increasingly used from the autumn of 1641 as an indication of Pym's prominence for the public and others at Westminster.

Pym's Junto: the term used for the idea that Pym and his allies, men like Denzil Holles, through their control of parliament had become the ruling power, a new government.

Fig. 2 '*King Pym*'

Key term

Recess: a temporary cessation of the sitting of parliament as a result of an adjournment, the postponement of the next meeting of either the Commons or Lords until a named date. In this break from their duties in parliament most MPs would return to their counties.

Key chronology

1641

February	Triennial Act.
May	Protestation Oath; army plot; death of Bedford.
10 May	Act of Attainder.
June	Ten Propositions.
	Abolition of Star Chamber; ship money made illegal.
August	Charles leaves for Scotland – the 'Incident'.
October/ November	Irish Rebellion; second army plot.
22–3 November	Grand Remonstrance, passes 159–148 votes.
	Charles returns to London.

1642

2 January	Charles offers Pym Chancellorship.
4 January	Five Members' Coup.
February	Henrietta Maria leaves England.
March	Militia Ordinance.
April	Charles attempts to seize the arsenal at Hull.
June	Nineteen Propositions; Charles issues commissions of array.
18 June	Answer to the Nineteen Propositions.
22 August	Nottingham: Charles raises his standard and civil war begins.

More clearly an attack on Pym was a letter delivered to him at the Commons in which he was called a bribe taker and a traitor. With the letter was a cloth that it was claimed had been dragged through a plague sore.

Pym took a leading role in ensuring that the Commons put financial pressure on Charles as a means to limit the King's political options. Pym did this by:

- only giving Charles income from tonnage and poundage on a two-monthly basis
- using committees to shape the policy of the Commons as a whole, notably the Recess Committee during the **recess** period from 9 September to 20 October.

The historian Morrill has argued that Pym's 'appointment as chair of the Recess Committee sealed his leadership role in developing an innovative parliamentary executive'. Hyde referred to Pym as being 'able to do most hurt' and an outsider, the Venetian ambassador, believed Pym was 'director of the whole machine'. Pym's influence stemmed from his criticism of Charles since 1626 but, more specifically, Pym's chairmanship of the Recess Committee. Conrad Russell's judgement that Pym was the most important figure in the Commons can be set against the other extreme of him being seen as merely a 'man of business' for influential peers who were leading a 'Noble Revolt'. Pym's influence lies somewhere in the middle. Morrill's qualification that Pym was merely prominent as the most visible figure of a wider opposition network indicates his importance alongside his allies.

For many contemporaries, however, Pym was important as he was the visible and vocal face of what seemed an increasingly far too radical attack on Charles' prerogative, coupled with a dangerous appeal outside parliament to the people.

> Even though by September 1641 the king had assented to all of parliament's demands, the reforming zeal of some members of parliament nevertheless remained. To a significant extent this was because the royal concessions had been accompanied with a palpable bad grace, raising a concern as to how far Charles could be trusted not to try to regain what he had conceded. Indeed this fear was crystallised in May 1641 when Pym revealed the Army Plot. In order to secure the concessions already obtained, Pym and his junto therefore sought, from May to November 1641, not simply to restrain the royal prerogative but to abrogate to parliament key aspects of it. These measures led some to support the king, encouraged to do so also because of the stance he had taken on religious issues.

4 *Seel, G. E. and Smith, D. L., **Crown and Parliaments**, 2001*

Thus Pym can be seen, and was seen by contemporaries, as a symbol of how parliament became more of a threat in 1641 to moderates than Charles. Pym should be seen in the context of the development of support for monarchy as moderates reacted to his stance in parliament. It was this that caused division, the formation of a royalist party and, most importantly therefore, the two sides necessary for a civil war in England.

The significance of the Grand Remonstrance and the development of support for the King

While the idea of a parliamentary opposition in the sense of an organised party may have been overstated, the unity of MPs started to dissolve when they had to consider what to replace the personal rule with. MPs could generally agree that they did not want a repeat of the personal rule, but how to prevent its repetition or what to put in its place brought into the open the differences in opinion that they had been happy to overlook in the context of what faced them in 1640. The breakdown of unity had begun when some regarded the use of an Act of Attainder to remove Wentworth as constitutionally dangerous. Religion caused further division. This development of division among MPs from the general unity that had existed in 1640 was the chief cause of the development of support for monarchy. Moderates became scared that the actions and beliefs of radicals such as Pym posed more of a threat to the political order than Charles I. This process has been labelled 'constitutional royalism'. Moderates supported monarchy and what it stood for rather than Charles as a reaction to parliamentary radicalism.

The potential support for the King, or rather a reaction in favour of monarchy in response to the radicalism of Charles' opponents, was the root of the development of a royalist party. Without this process, civil war would not have been possible as there would not have been the two sides to fight it. The radicalism of parliament seemed to be confirmed by their Ten Propositions of 24 June 1641. In this document it was made clear that for settlement to be achieved the King would need to accept limitations of his power, including the following:

- Parliamentary input into who was in his Privy Council.
- Control of those around the Queen.
- Parliamentary control over religious education for the royal children.

There was little chance that Charles would agree to such restrictions.

In Scotland, there was also a reaction as many felt radicals in the covenanting alliance had gone too far too fast. In August 1640, the Earl of Montrose and 17 other Scottish nobles signed the Cumbernauld Band stating a desire to defend the King. This was a significant division in Scotland. Charles appreciated that an agreement with some leading Scots would remove the main prop for his opponents in the long parliament, the occupying Scottish army. To play on this division, Charles chose to accept the abolition of episcopacy in Scotland and the Scottish reforms to date.

Key profile

James Graham, 1st Marquis and 5th Earl of Montrose

As well as being a leading member of the Scottish nobility, Montrose (1612–50) took a leading role in the Scottish Kirk in opposing the imposition of Laudianism. He signed the National Covenant and fought in their armies in 1639 and 1640. His concern at the religious radicalism of others in the covenanting movement, especially the Earl of Argyll, led him to see Charles as a means of stopping the Scottish Revolution going further.

Exploring the detail

Constitutional royalism

This was a reaction by moderates who, although they may have been concerned or even opposed to Charles' policies in the 1630s, were more worried by the development of a parliamentary radicalism since 1640, exemplified by Pym, and the apparent growing threat of social order across the country. In the face of radical Puritanism, parliament taking over the prerogative of the crown and the power of the mob many nobles and gentry looked to monarchy, rather than Charles, as the best protection for a moderate Protestant Church, law, order and their continued influence.

Activity

Thinking point

Why would Charles I be unlikely to agree to the terms of the Ten Propositions?

■ **Activity**

Revision exercise

1 What kind of 'evidence' from 1625 onwards could Pym have presented to the Commons to suggest that Charles I was likely to have been implicated in the 'Incident'?

For help with this task, go back through the book and construct a 'charge sheet' of Charles' actions to show that he could not be trusted.

2 From this list, write a speech in the manner in which you think Pym would deliver this 'evidence' to the House of Commons.

To take advantage of this reaction, the King arrived in Scotland in August 1641. The Commons' distrust of Charles is shown by the organisation of a parliamentary committee of defence to send commissioners, one of whom was Hampden, to keep an eye on Charles in Scotland. The question as to whether Charles should be accompanied to Scotland also indicates growing division in parliament. This was seen in the vote of 8 November 1641, proposed by Pym, that commissioners be sent to Scotland to watch over Charles. Charles' position in Scotland and England was, however, undermined by the 'Incident'.

The 'Incident' was an attempt, while Charles was in Scotland, by the more extreme royalists, for example the Earl of Crawford, but also moderate covenanters, like Montrose, to seize leading radical covenanter leaders like Argyll. It was believed that Charles was implicated in this plot, a belief that he reinforced by attending the Edinburgh parliament on 12 October accompanied by an armed force. The 'Incident' destroyed Charles' hopes of gaining further support in Scotland. When Charles left Scotland on 17 November 1641, he had to appoint his opponents to key posts. Just as Charles arrived back in Westminster his position got much worse; news had broken of the Irish Rebellion.

The Irish Rebellion

In the development of support for monarchy the key period was after the Irish Rebellion of October 1641. Wentworth had succeeded in alienating all the different groups in Ireland. The Scottish Revolution and Wentworth's return to England prompted the Irish Catholics to act. Faced by Presbyterian Scots controlling Scotland who were in contact with Puritans like Pym in England who seemed to be growing in influence, the removal of Wentworth's authority seemed to offer the opportunity for a pre-emptive strike before radical Protestants in Scotland and England sought to impose even harsher rule on Catholic Ireland.

In explaining why the Irish rebelled and the consequent impact of this rebellion upon politics at Westminster, the historian Conrad Russell referred to the 'billiard-ball effect'. By this, he meant that the Irish Rebellion was prompted by events in Scotland and England but, in turn, the Irish Rebellion radicalised the situation in England.

Perceptions of the Irish Rebellion in England were more important politically than in reality. Fear of Catholicism and the imminent invasion of the forces of the anti-Christ, i.e. Catholic armies, were heightened by the accounts of survivors and the distorted images of the massacres produced in the press.

■ **Activity**

Thinking point

What impact would accounts such as that in Source 5 have in England?

> The Rebels daily increase in men, exercising all manner of cruelties, and striving who can be most barbarously exquisite in tormenting the poor Protestants wheresoever they come, cutting off their privy members, ears, fingers and hands, plucking out their eyes, boiling the heads of little children before their Mothers' faces, and then ripping up their Mothers' bowels; stripping women naked, killing the children as soon as they are born, and ripping up their Mothers' bellies as soon as they are delivered; driving men, women and children by hundreds upon Bridges and from thence cast them down into Rivers.

5   *Letter from Thomas Partington, settler in Ireland, to a friend in England, read out in the Commons*

Fig. 3 *Later depiction of torture of Protestants*

Even a conservative commentator such as Clarendon thought that 40,000 Protestants had been killed in Ireland. Even recent assessments still range widely from 3,000 to 12,000 killed over the winter of 1641–2.

The Irish Rebellion radicalised politics at Westminster because the anti-Catholicism of most in England and many in parliament, especially Puritans like Pym, made them, in turn, fear a Catholic invasion and determined to avenge the massacre of Protestants in Ireland. As the historian Morrill has shown in the early months of 1642, Pym's 'obsession was with Ireland'.

The Irish Rebellion also came in the context of previous fears of the supposed plan by which Wentworth would bring the English army in Ireland to England for Charles' use against his enemies. The most important question raised by the Irish Rebellion was not whether an army would be sent to Ireland but could Charles I be trusted with it. This issue would force the question of allegiance upon MPs but also make Pym and his allies take more radical action.

■ Cross-reference

For an explanation of the **Militia Bill** see page 128.

■ Did you know?

A key issue about the Grand Remonstrance was the question whether to print it and thereby allow the people access to political debate and criticism of the monarch. One of Charles I's objections to the 1628 Petition of Right had been on the same grounds. In 1641, the proposal to print the Grand Remonstrance led to chaos on the floor of the Commons and the only time in our history when swords were drawn in parliament.

The significance of the Grand Remonstrance

At the start of November 1641 Pym introduced the Grand Remonstrance to the Commons. This was a list of criticisms of Charles' government since 1625, which, for Pym, clearly showed why the King could not be trusted with control of the army that needed to be raised to crush the Irish Rebellion. Moderates were alarmed by the Grand Remonstrance's language and content. It had a particular virulent anti-Catholicism, which for the historian Fletcher 'takes us directly into the inner recesses of Pym's mind'. For many, the idea of using the Grand Remonstrance as an appeal to the people to put pressure on those who had up to that point opposed the Militia Bill was dangerously radical.

The significance of the Grand Remonstrance comes from the following:

1 It was a direct attack on Charles.
2 Political issues were being deliberately and openly targeted out of Westminster to directly involve the people as a means of exerting pressure on MPs.
3 The debate as to whether to publish the Grand Remonstrance shows real division in parliament and, as a result, the basis of two sides by which a civil war might be fought.

> Pym and his allies sought to make use of the City's political, financial, and military resources to achieve their own program with a minimum of socio-political disruption. They were willing to countenance revolution in the City, but only when this became indispensible to ensure that London's resources would be put at Parliament's disposal. They accepted autonomous action by the popular masses, but only as a necessary evil, for it posed a real threat, not only to their own fundamental conceptions of order and hierarchy, but to the short-term requirements of maintaining the support of as many as possible of the country's easily frightened gentry. As it was, the turn to London symbolised by the printing of the Grand Remonstrance probably lost Pym and his friends something like half of their former allies in Parliament.

 *Brenner, R., **Merchants and Revolution. Commercial Change, Political Conflict, and London's Overseas Traders, 1550–1653**, 1993*

■ Activity

Thinking point

What was the concern about giving Charles control of an army?

The debate on the Grand Remonstrance lasted 12 hours. The significance of the eventual vote at two o'clock on the morning of 23 November lies in that the Grand Remonstrance was passed by only 159 votes to 148. Nothing illustrates more how parliament had become divided since 1640. The votes against the Grand Remonstrance, coupled with the many MPs who had already left parliament, show that a royalist party was a reality and, thus, the two sides necessary for a civil war in England had emerged. Therefore, Charles' position undermined by the Irish Rebellion was strengthened as moderates reacted to the radicalism of the Grand Remonstrance and the immediate need to address the question of who should command the army to be sent to Ireland.

This question of who should command the army that all agreed should be raised to crush the Catholic rebels was a key source of division in parliament. The Irish Rebellion had further weakened trust in Charles, as one of its leaders, Sir Phelim O'Neill, had claimed to be acting in his name, producing a forged royal warrant to that effect. To avenge the deaths of thousands of Protestants an army would have to be raised, which should by his prerogative be under the command of the King.

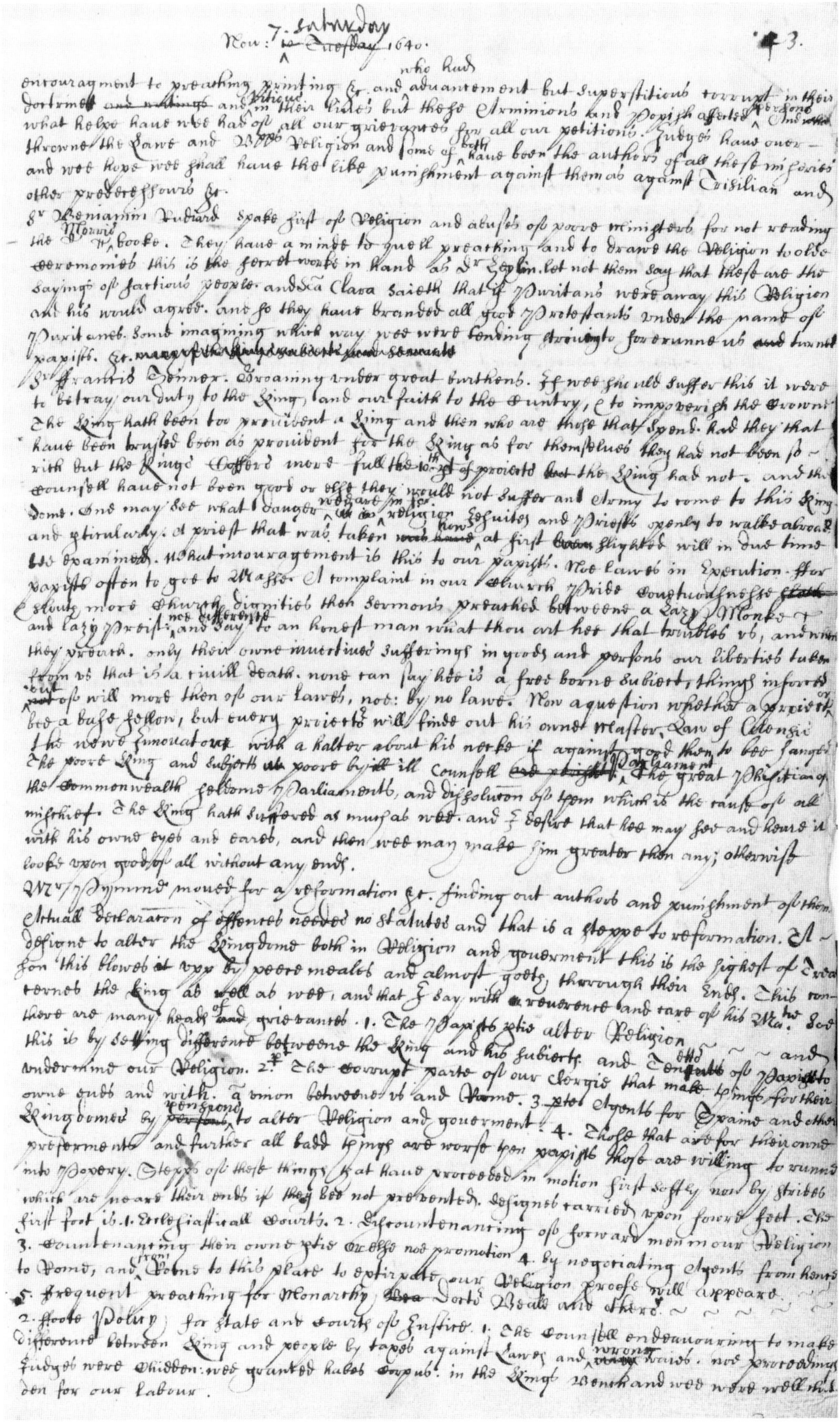
Nov: 7. Saturday 1640. 43.

encouragment to preaching printing &c. and advancement but superstitious corrupt in their doctrines and in their lives but these Arminians and Popish affected persons. And what helpe have wee had of all our grievances for all our petitions. Judges have overthrowne the Lawe and Bishops Religion and some of both have been the authors of all these mischeifes and wee hope wee shall have the like punishment against them as against Trisilian and other predecessours &c.

Sr Benjamin Rudiard spake first of Religion and abuses of poore ministers for not reading the Booke. They have a minde to quell preaching and to drawe the Religion to olde Ceremonies this is the forest worke in hand as Dr Heylin. let not them say that these are the sayings of factious people. and Sa Clara saieth that if Puritans were away this Religion and his would agree. and so they have branded all good Protestants under the name of Puritanes. Some imagining which way wee were bending strainge to overrunne us and turne papists. &c.

Sr Francis Seymer. Groaning under great burthens. If wee should suffer this it were to betray our duty to the King, and our faith to the Country, & to impoverish the Crowne. The King hath been too provident a King and then who are those that spend. had they that have been trusted been as provident for the King as for themselves they had not been so rich but the Kings Coffers more full the 10th of projects but the King had not. and the counsell have not been good or else they would not suffer an Army to come to this Kingdome. One may see what danger wee are in for religion Jesuites and Priests openly to walke abroad and particularly: A priest that was taken here at first slighted will in due time be examined. What incouragement is this to our papists. Noe Lawes in Execution. For papists often to goe to Masse. A complaint in our Church Pride Covetousnesse sloth more Church dignities then Sermons preached betweene a Lazy Monke and lazy Priest: not different and say to an honest man what thou art hee that troubles us, and when they preach. only their owne invented sufferings in goods and persons our liberties taken from us that is a civill death. none can say hee is a free borne subiect, things inforced out of will more then of our Lawes, not: by no lawe. Now a question whether a priest or bee a base fellow, but every priest will finde out his owne Master, Law of Clergie the newe Innovatour with a halter about his necke if against good then to bee hanged. The poore King and subiects poore by ill counsell parliament. The great Phisitian of the Commonwealth followed Parliaments, and dissolution of them which is the cause of all mischief. The King hath suffered as much as wee. and I desire that hee may see and heare it with his owne eyes and eares, and then wee may make him greater then any; otherwise looke upon good of all without any ends.

Mr Pymme moved for a reformation &c. finding out authors and punishment of them. Actuall declaration of offences needed no statutes and that is a stoppe to reformation. A designe to alter the Kingdome both in Religion and government this is the highest of treason this blowes at upp by poore mealles and almost goods, through their ends. This concernes the King as well as wee, and that I say with reverence and care of his Matie. See there are many heads of grievances. 1. The Papists Plot alter Religion this is by setting difference betweene the King and his subiects. and ~ ~ and undermine our Religion. 2d The corrupt parte of our Clergie that make things for Papists to owne ends and with a union betweene us and Rome. 3. Their Agents for Kingdomes by correspond, to alter Religion and government. 4. Those that are for their owne preferments and further all bad things are worse then papists those are willing to runne into Popery. Steppes of these things that have proceeded in motion first softly now by strides which are neare their ends if they bee not prevented. designes carried upon foure feet. The first foot is 1. Ecclesiasticall Courts. 2. Discountenancing of forward men in our Religion 3. Countenancing their owne not promotion 4. by negotiating Agents from hence to Rome, and from Rome to this place to extirpate our Religion proofes will appeare. 5. frequent preaching for Monarchy Doctr Beale and others. ~ ~ ~

2. foote Policy for state and courts of Justice. 1. The Counsell endeavouring to make difference betweene King and people by cases against Lawes and wrongs. not proceedings Judges were chidden: wee granted habeas corpus. in the Kings Bench and wee were well chidden for our labour.

Fig. 4 *Parliamentary journal of Sir Simonds d'Ewes, c1640*

For some, Charles' actions to date raised the question whether he could be trusted with the command of an army.

What forced MPs to take sides on who should command the army was the introduction of the Militia Bill.

The Militia Bill

In a forerunner of the Militia Bill in early November Pym had introduced an 'additional instruction' that if parliament was going to help raise an army to subdue Ireland, Charles should only appoint councillors approved by parliament. Pym only won this vote by 151 votes to 110. Even a strong Protestant like Sir Simonds D'Ewes voted against it. On 7 December 1641, Sir Arthur Haselrig introduced the Militia Bill to remove the King's power over the trained bands completely and give parliament the power to appoint army commanders. The Militia Bill then essentially proposed that parliament would be in control of the army raised to crush the Irish rebels.

Key profile

Sir Arthur Haselrig

Haselrig (1610–61) was a Puritan who, because of his role in attacking Laud, his involvement in Wentworth's attainder, the Root and Branch Petition and the Militia Bill, was selected as one of the Five Members for arrest by Charles I.

Activity

Source analysis

What does Source 7 indicate about how Charles viewed the Militia Ordinance?

We cannot but observe the strange exorbitant power which the two Houses at this time, misled by a few factious, malicious spirits, pretend to transfer to themselves, and by which the Militia is put in execution; it being so supreme and absolute, that our consent is not thought necessary for the execution of anything they judge to be convenient for the welfare of the kingdom.

7   *Charles I to Lord Willoughby of Parham*

With the intense division over the Grand Remonstrance and Militia, rather than wait for more parliamentarians to side with monarchy, Charles decided that the time was ripe to seize the leaders of the parliamentary opposition. What also motivated Charles was that, while he may have been gaining support, his political position at Westminster was undermined by the Lords accepting a Commons vote of impeachment against the bishops on 29 December, thereby potentially leading to their removal and the loss of significant royalist support in the Lords. In deciding on a coup, Charles showed that he still regarded parliament as being subverted by a small radical group, chiefly motivated by their Puritanism. In December, Charles appointed the royalist hardliner Colonel Thomas Lunsford to command the Tower signalling the continued possibility that he might stage a coup. At the start of January 1642, Charles staged one.

Charles' attempted coup was a complete failure. On 3 January 1642, Charles announced the impeachment of Pym, Hampden, Haselrig, Holles, William Strode and Edward Montagu, Lord Kimbolton. The next day he entered the Commons with a force to arrest them but found that they, forewarned, had left.

Fig. 5 *The Tower of London*

The Five Members' Coup was a mistake too far. Pym could easily use it as further proof of the danger Charles posed and that the King could not be negotiated with. More seriously, the attempted coup also led to popular demonstrations against Charles, which so shook him that he felt compelled to take his family from London to Hampton Court for their safety. The next time Charles was in London was for his public execution seven years later in 1649. By leaving the capital, Charles in effect gave control of London to parliament. The physical division of King and parliament made negotiation more difficult and was illustrative of the drift to conflict.

Key term

Exclusion Bill: this removed the bishops from the House of Lords and thus lessened the influence of the King.

Exploring the detail

The Militia Ordinance

This appointed lord lieutenants and their deputies by the authority of parliament without the royal assent. It was named an Ordinance, rather than an Act. By this measure, parliament assumed control of the armed forces.

Activity

Thinking point

How important was Pym in the growth of support for

1 the King

2 the Grand Remonstrance

3 the Militia Ordinance?

Exploring the detail

Commissions of array

In response to the Militia Ordinance, Charles invoked a prerogative means of raising forces last used in the early 1500s. Commissions of array were sent to leading figures in the counties authorising them to raise forces for the crown.

Activity

Talking point

As a class, discuss whether you would have accepted parliament's Militia Ordinance or Charles I's commissions of array.

Charles' attempted coup strengthened the position of parliamentary radicals who pushed for:

- the removal of 'evil councillors'
- parliamentary approval of the commanders of the Militia, forts, and the Tower
- an **Exclusion Bill**, preventing bishops sitting in the House of Lords.

Popular support for this programme was encouraged by a petitioning campaign. At the end of December a petition calling for the removal of bishops from parliament had 30,000 signatures. The Earl of Huntingdon left an account of the pressure the Lords came under from the people of London:

> Ten thousand were between York House and Charing Cross with staves and some swords. They stood so thick that we had much ado to pass with our coaches, and though it were a dark night their innumerable number of links made it as light as day. They cried, 'No bishops' and looked in our coaches whether any bishops were therein, that we went in great danger.

Popular demonstrations in London put pressure especially on the Lords and on 5 February 1642 they accepted an Exclusion Bill.

On 15 February the Militia Bill was finally issued as an Ordinance, passed solely by the authority of parliament without Charles' approval on 5 March 1642.

To support the Militia Ordinance, parliament ironically proposed the raising of £400,000 by the ship money formula.

Charles' own actions again helped the radicals in parliament. Charles' attempt to seize the military supplies at Hull clearly sent a different message to that of the constitutional royalist propaganda. The central issue for the country after Charles left London was whether to accept parliament's Militia Ordinance or Charles' equally legally dubious commissions of array.

On the basis of these measures, both parliament and Charles prepared for civil war.

Summary questions

1 Write two obituaries for Pym as if he had died in November 1641. One should be written as if it would appear in a royalist paper, and the other as if it would appear in a parliamentary paper.

2 Construct a chart based on the information in this chapter. List the evidence that illustrates how Charles I's position was undermined and how it was strengthened.

The causes of the English Civil War

Fig. 1 *Battle of Edgehill, Warwickshire, 23 October 1642*

In this chapter you will learn about:

- the reasons behind the outbreak of the Civil War

- the problems caused by Britain's 'multiple kingdoms'

- the notion of 'constitutional royalism'.

Lord Falkland was, alongside Hyde and Colepeper, one of the most prominent constitutional royalists. These men, like the moderate majority all across the country, did not want a civil war. In 1643, one year into the conflict, Falkland's despair was such that he was determined to end his life. At the battle of Newbury, Falkland volunteered to serve and deliberately charged on horseback into the firing parliamentarian line to be instantly killed. Why had England descended into civil war when such men as Falkland, but more importantly, the majority of the country, had not wanted conflict?

The reasons for the outbreak of the English Civil War

There were a number of issues, themes and events that came together in the period from the Scottish Revolution of July 1637 to early 1642 that can be seen as the reasons for the outbreak of the Civil War in England.

- Multiple kingdoms.
- Constitutional royalism.
- Charles I.
- Religion.

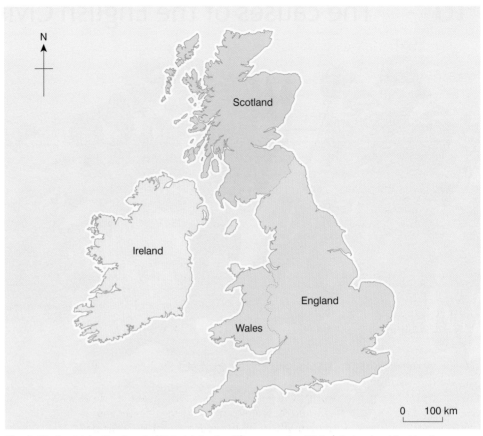

Fig. 2 *The 'multiple-kingdoms' of 'Britain': England (incorporating Wales), Ireland and Scotland*

Multiple kingdoms

Although 'the British Problem' has been used to describe the problem of England's relationship with Scotland and Ireland, it is probably better, given the place of Ireland within this issue, to look at this as the problem of ruling 'multiple kingdoms'. Charles I was King of England, which incorporated Wales, King of Scotland and King of Ireland. He therefore faced the practical difficulties that also beset other European multiple-monarchies. What was different and more complex about his situation was the religious divisions in and between the kingdoms. Charles' personality and policies, notably the attempt to impose uniformity, exacerbated these religious tensions. The Scottish Revolution of 1637 was provoked by religion. Religion was clearly a factor in the outbreak of the Irish Rebellion and religion was a factor in how Englishmen reacted to their crisis of 1641 to 1642.

> There can be no doubt that the religious imperialism of King Charles, the attempt to create a uniformity of worship or at least of order in the Church throughout his three kingdoms, was at best provocative, at worst destructive, not only of the religious independence of the three kingdoms, but potentially of the monarchy itself.

1   *Bennett, M.,* ***The English Civil War****, 1995*

Furthermore, the kingdoms interacted with each other. Conrad Russell's term 'the billiard-ball effect' is a comment on how the Scottish Revolution impacted on England, both of which in turn impacted on Ireland, and then how the Irish Rebellion impacted on England and Scotland.

The conflicts that broke out in Scotland, Ireland and England in part reflected potential sources of stress that can be traced back over several decades, and they were profoundly affected by the fact that each kingdom was part of a composite monarchy. Such long term structural problems help to explain why a crisis of some kind befell the early Stuart monarchies. Yet they cannot tell the whole story. It is an obvious but highly significant point that the crisis did not come under James I but under Charles I. Unlike James, his son upset delicate balances and enflamed areas of tension. In so far Charles had a 'British' policy, he sought not to unify his three kingdoms but to assert his personal authority in each of them. In the end, it was primarily his policies and his authoritarian style of government that brought about the 'fall of the British monarchies'.

2

> Smith, D. L., *A History of the Modern British Isles,*
> *1603–1707,* 1998

It can be seen then that it was not just the problem of multiple kingdoms that produced civil war in England. The fact that these multiple kingdoms were all ruled by Charles I was crucial. Charles' brand of kingship brought tension in and between all kingdoms to a head.

Yet, no matter the importance of the Scottish or Irish rebellions, civil war did not break out in England until August 1642. Charles' position was strengthened by the attempts to deal with the issues raised by these rebellions. The vote on the Grand Remonstrance and the debate over the Militia Bill indicated that constitutional royalism meant that there was more support for Charles than there had appeared in 1640.

Constitutional royalism

Discussion of the Militia Bill's direct questioning of Charles' prerogative and attempt to transfer it to parliament prompted further splits in the broad parliamentary alliance that came in to place in 1640.

In December 1641, in his public statements, Charles was able to pose increasingly convincingly as defender of the 'fundamental law' against the revolutionaries, a key example being The King's Answer to the Petition accompanying the Grand Remonstrance of 23 December 1641. Charles' positioning of himself as the defender of the constitution succeeded in winning over 'constitutional royalists' like Hyde, Falkland and Colepeper. They, in turn, reinforced Charles' tendency to continue this presentation of himself and what he stood for as constitutional royalism, furthering the development of a royalist party.

> Royalists fought for the traditions of religion and monarchy that their ancestors had preserved and passed on to them. They believed in bishops and the divine right of kings not so much as intellectual propositions than as the moorings of a hierarchy in church and state. Their fundamental principle was loyalty – an instinct deeply etched in the patriarchal nature of their society. Disloyalty was base. Devotion was the emotive force behind the King's cause.

3

> Kishlansky, M., *A Monarchy Transformed. Britain*
> *1603–1714,* 1997

Activity

Revision exercise

Using bullet points and Source 3, summarise the reasons given for royalism.

Kishlansky, as others, therefore sees constitutional royalism as essentially conservative. Fearful of the apparent growing influence of radicals like Pym in parliament, many began to see Charles as the best protection of order. All that maintained their position in society was linked to monarchy. If loyalty to Charles completely collapsed, what was to stop those lower in society rebelling against those above them?

> Constitutional Royalism was a cluster of interdependent ideas whose secular and religious aspects can be distinguished but not separated. The beliefs that the royal prerogative and the subjects' liberties operated in symbiosis; that the monarch's powers were sovereign yet consistent with the rule of law; that to abrogate those powers therefore violated both the constitution and the laws; that monarchy and episcopacy were bound together by the royal supremacy enshrined in statute – all these components meshed to form one coherent whole. If there was a single principle underpinning these ideas, holding them in equilibrium, it was the rule of law. It was guided by a temperate spirit which saw unity and reciprocity as the normative relationship between monarch and people, Crown and Parliament, Church and State. In that sense, it was an outlook rather than an ideology, a frame of mind rather than creed.

4 *Smith, D. L., **Constitutional Royalism and the Search for Settlement, c.1640–1649**, 1994*

Activity

Source analysis

How far do Sources 3 and 4 disagree in their interpretation of what motivated some royalists?

Even a committed parliamentarian like Sir John Hotham, who was to refuse the King entry to the arsenal at Hull in April 1642, was concerned at the power parliament and Pym were taking to themselves.

On 2 June 1642, parliament issued The Nineteen Propositions, their demands for a negotiated settlement, which indicated the extent of power they felt they needed.

On 18 June 1642, Falkland and Colepeper produced the Answer to the Nineteen Propositions for the King as a response.

Activity

Revision exercise

List examples of parliament's measures that increasingly concerned men like Hotham.

Key profile

Lucius Cary, 2nd Viscount Falkland

Falkland (1610–43) fought for Charles I in the First Bishops' War of 1639, before being elected to the short and long parliaments. In parliament, Falkland spoke against both Laud and Strafford, as well as supporting the abolition of ship money and the passage of the Triennial Act. His drift towards constitutional royalism seems to have come from a fear of the consequences of the Root and Branch Petition and the Grand Remonstrance. Falkland was persuaded to join the King by Hyde. For Falkland, the priority was always to achieve a settlement with parliament, which he believed would be possible with negotiation. He despaired at the onset of conflict. In 1643, at the Battle of Newbury, Falkland committed suicide by deliberately riding into musket fire.

The Nineteen Propositions

- All privy councillors are to be approved by parliament.
- The five members are to be pardoned.
- Charles has to accept the Triennial Act and Militia Ordinance.
- Parliament will direct a reformation of the Church.

Fig. 3 *The Nineteen Propositions*

The Answer to The Nineteen Propositions was the classic statement of constitutional royalism. It portrayed the King as the force that would prevent anarchy. Parliament's proposals would lead to 'a dark equal chaos of confusion' where the threat of popular rebellion was imminent. The desire for moderation in religion was also central to constitutional royalism. It was claimed that Catholicism would be rooted out but also the Puritan radicalism that appeared to have been let loose by parliament's undermining of Charles' authority. Falkland and Colepeper wrote that the King would defend the Church of England.

> ...with constancy maintain in their purity and glory, not only against all invasions of popery, but also from the irreverence of those many schismaticks and separatists wherewith of late this kingdom and our City of London abounds.

5   *The Answer to The Nineteen Propositions*

It is clear that constitutional royalism was as religious as it was political. In the 17th century, politics and religion were one.

> A growing number of peers and greater gentry feared that the intervention of popular forces menaced the ruling class, and they turned to the king as the symbol and defender of social order. He insisted on maintaining the Episcopal government and the existing liturgy of the church. They were prepared to accept that because they were panicked by the appearance, though on a small scale as yet, of Protestant sects which rejected the established church altogether, and of radical elements hostile to the existing social order.

6   *Manning, B.,* **Aristocrats, Plebians and Revolution in England 1640–1660,** *1996*

The crucial importance of constitutional royalism is that without it Charles would not have had the support with which to fight a civil war in England. Such was the shift of moderates it is even possible that civil war could have been avoided. That civil war was not avoided was down to what had been the root cause of the start of the crisis in 1637, Charles I.

Charles I

It is significant that in the complex historiography of the causes of the Civil War the one thing almost all historians can agree on is that Charles was not a good king and that he made conflict much more likely. He was the key factor.

Charles I's most recent academic biographer, Cust, has even reiterated the point that his strengths were actually political weaknesses.

> In the end it was Charles' strengths as much as his weaknesses that brought disaster. Had he simply been incompetent he could have been deposed or reduced to a figurehead. It was his capacity to recover, and form a party, after first alienating the bulk of the political nation, which produced a civil war.

7   *Cust, R.,* **Charles I,** *2006*

 Activity

Group activity

In pairs, write a justification for Charles accepting The Nineteen Propositions and a justification for Charles not accepting them.

 Activity

Thinking point

1   What was wrong with Charles I?

2   Construct a chart listing Charles' strengths and weaknesses as a king.

Fig. 4 *Charles I's masked executioner waits with his axe*

Charles was hampered from the very start. He was James I's second son and was therefore never supposed to be king. Charles' elder brother, Henry, was everything a king was supposed to be in the early modern period and everything that Charles was not.

Physically strong, clever, a good communicator and a strong Protestant, Henry was a hard act to follow. There is clearly an element of the glorification of Henry being more a reaction to his early death at the age of 16 and as a criticism of his father than an exact reality, but Henry does seem to have had the making of a strong monarch. Charles, literally, did not measure up. Indeed Charles' inferiority complex was a reaction to his poor relationship with his father, the obvious strengths of his elder brother and the influence of Buckingham. Charles came to the throne as a slow, stammering, pedantic young man determined to enforce his prerogative as a mask for his own shortcomings.

Charles I was ill-suited to cope with his plight, and must rank amongst the most inept of all English kings. While it would be foolish to conclude that the Civil War occurred simply because Charles was king, it would be equally foolish to underestimate the part played by his personality.

8   *Hirst, D., **Authority and Conflict: England 1603–58**, 1985*

Charles was not stupid, but his mind was narrow and inflexible, and since his imagination was severely limited he too often failed to foresee the results of his decisions or to gauge their impact on other people. Indeed decisions did not come easily to him, and once he had painfully arrived at them he tended to affirm them so uncompromisingly that if a tactical withdrawal should prove necessary, as it often did, it was bound to be humiliating.

9   *Woolrych, A.,* **Britain in Revolution**, *2002*

The obvious example of Charles' actions creating opposition to him and hastening conflict is the Five Members' Coup of January 1642. Just as his support was consolidating, Charles' precipitate action allowed parliament to push through the Militia Ordinance.

The Civil War did not break out in March 1642 with the passage of the Militia Ordinance. The majority on both sides still wished to avoid war. Across the country the gentry in 22 counties, a prominent example being Yorkshire, attempted to prevent war by using the kinship ties that bound them to construct neutrality pacts. These attempts at preventing war could not counter the actions of more determined men who were more driven. Armed conflict resulted as radicals on both sides tried to get control of local stores of ammunition in preparation for war. These radicals were chiefly motivated by religion.

Religion

Religion created opposition because of Charles I's determination to enforce Laudianism. The Scottish Revolution or the imposition of Laudianism would not have been likely without Charles I. Charles I was the main cause of civil war in England. What most determined which side people lined up with was, however, religion.

Fig. 5 *Henry, Prince of Wales, brother of Charles I*

What turned constitutional opposition to an unconstitutional taking up of arms? What made men throughout England in 1642 decide to impose terms upon the king by force, rather than using the power of parliamentary supply to get the best settlement the king would grant? While many distrusted the king in 1642 and wanted further guarantees of his future conduct, it was principally those who also believed in the necessity of a second Reformation who determined to fight.

10   *Morrill, J.,* **The Nature of the English Revolution**, *1993*

Although there had been attempts to avoid religious discussion, early in the long parliament it is clear that religion was a real source of division. The debate on the Root and Branch Petition of 8–9 February 1641 was bitter. Significantly, as Smith has stated, 'no other debate so accurately prefigured subsequent political allegiance at so early a date'. The three most notable constitutional royalists, Hyde, Falkland and Colepeper,

Activity

Thinking point

What kind of people are being referred to in Source 10? From your own reading of this section, give an example of an individual who may fit this description.

Cross-reference

To learn more about **Oliver Cromwell** as a parliamentarian, see page 139.

all wanted just minor reform to the episcopacy. Oliver Cromwell was a prominent supporter of Root and Branch. When the Commons introduced a bill for abolishing episcopacy in May 1641, the vote on 27 May as to whether it should receive a second reading was 139 to 108.

Religion was a key factor across all of three kingdoms.

> Religion is generally seen as the most important factor in determining popular allegiance in all three kingdoms; and in Scotland and Ireland there were powerful groups that justified the resort to arms partly in terms of a holy war against Antichrist. Many English people, including future royalists, were worried not so much by Charles' preference for 'popish' religious forms as by his self-proclaimed authority to make changes in religion without recourse to Parliament. The Covenanters, by contrast, based their defiance of Charles largely upon the duty of a covenanted nation to fulfil God's design. It was only when the English looked to the struggle in Ireland that they thought in terms of a war of religion.

11 Scott, D., *Politics and War in the Three Stuart Kingdoms, 1637–49*, 2004

Events away from the English parliament at Westminster had an impact on the moderates. Not only were men like Hyde concerned by the Presbyterianism of the Scots and Pym's links with them, but also with the evidence of the growing popular radicalism across the country. Economic riots as well as **iconoclasm** were exactly why, for moderates, the Church needed to be maintained as another prop to order.

Activity

Talking point

Read the previous two paragraphs again. Construct a paragraph to mirror Morrill's writing in Source 10 – outlining how religion was also a reason for some supporting Charles I and monarchy.

Even Sir Edward Dering, who had introduced the Root and Branch Petition, retreated to moderation when made aware of iconoclasm in his native Kent. The iconoclasm of the period was also associated with social breakdown, which pushed moderates towards monarchy as a prop to order. In Hingham, Norfolk local 'ruffians' were bribed with drink to destroy the outward signs of Laudianism in the local church.

Iconoclasm was also linked with fear of the increasing influence of Pym and the radicals in parliament. It was Pym who brought a resolution through the Commons in September 1641, encouraging iconoclasm against popish images and altar rails. What

Fig. 6 *The soldiers in their passage to York turn into reformers as they pull down popish pictures, break down rails and turn altars into tables*

also alarmed moderates about this was the fact that the Commons acted on their own authority.

It was in response to such fears that Charles' positioning himself as a constitutional royalist, who had disowned Laudianism and was actually appointing moderate Calvinists, appealed so much. The King appeared less of a threat than Pym and his allies. Ann Hughes has argued that in 1641–2 'commitment to the "established" church and opposition to religious radicalism became central to the emerging royalist "party"'.

While the reaction to religious radicalism led many who had supported parliament in 1640 to become royalists, it was their religious radicalism that made others continue to support parliament. Two differing examples of this are Sir Simonds D'Ewes and Oliver Cromwell.

A closer look

What made a parliamentarian?

In many ways, Simonds D'Ewes was a natural constitutional royalist. A Suffolk MP, D'Ewes was politically moderate. He left the house at the time of the Grand Remonstrance and Five Members' Coup. But what was most important for D'Ewes was religion. Thus, despite his fear of radicalism, he felt he had no choice but to join parliament in the struggle against popery.

In the years 1653 to 1658, Oliver Cromwell was Lord Protector, ruler of England, conqueror of Scotland and Ireland. In 1640, Cromwell entered parliament as probably the poorest MP and, although linked to men like Hampden, a minor figure. Like D'Ewes, religion was central to Cromwell's life. Unlike D'Ewes, religion for Cromwell was a driving force that made him act. Cromwell was one of those motivated by religion who took action to organise troops and seize arms in the period of 'phoney war' between March and August 1642.

Fig. 7 *Oliver Cromwell*

This motivated minority on both sides was critical in 1642.

The moderate majority in the provinces was usually disorganized and indecisive, and it was this paralysis of will that in most counties allowed the minority of activists to seize the initiative. These activists were those who felt most strongly about religion. In the end, moderate Royalists and moderate Parliamentarians could not unite during the summer of 1642 because the former mistrusted Pym more than Charles, whereas the latter mistrusted Charles more than Pym.

12   *Smith, D. L., **A History of the Modern British Isles,** 1603–1707, 1998*

A true and exact Relation of the
manner of his Maiesties setting up of His
Standard at *Nottingham*, on Munday the
22. of August 1642.

First, The forme of the Standard, as it is here figured , and who were present at the advancing of it

Secondly, The danger of setting up of former Standards , and the damage
which ensued thereon.

Thirdly, A relation of all the Standards that ever were set up by any King.

Fourthly, the names of those Knights who are appointed to be the Kings
Standard-bearers. With the forces that are appoynted to guard it.

Fifthly, The manner of the Kings comming first to *Coventry*.

Sixtly, The *Cavalieres* resolution and dangerous threats which they have
uttered, if the King concludes a peace without them. or hearkens unto
his great Councell the Parliament : Moreover how they have shared
and divided *London* amongst themselves already.

Fig. 8 *A pamphlet recording the setting up of Charles I's standard*

Charles I officially declared war on parliament by raising his standard at Nottingham on 22 August 1642.

At Edgehill, in October 1642, the first major battle of the English Civil War took place.

The outbreak of civil war in England was due to a number of factors that combined together to produce conflict. The multiple-kingdom dimension was clearly important, with both the Scottish Revolution of 1637 and the Irish Rebellion of 1641 having a radicalising effect on English politics. What is clear, however, is that it still took a lot to push Englishmen to fight each other. Those most committed religiously were more prepared to take action. Underpinning both of these reasons, however, is the central role of Charles I. It was he who sparked the Scottish Revolution. His policies in Ireland contributed to the outbreak of rebellion there. His imposition of Laudianism had radicalised English Puritans. Without Charles I, civil war in England would have been much less likely.

> When three kingdoms under one ruler all take to armed resistance within three years, it seems sensible to investigate the possibility that their actions may have had some common causes. There are two obvious types of cause which are common to all three kingdoms. One is that they were all ruled by Charles I. The other thing all three kingdoms have in common is that they are all part of multiple kingdoms, all of which were internally divided in religion, and in all of which there existed a powerful group which preferred the religion of one of the others to their own. Charles, at some date not later than 1633 decided to drop a match into this powder keg by setting out to achieve one uniform order of religion within the three kingdoms.

 Russell, C., *The British Problem and the English Civil War*, 1987

Activity

Source analysis

What three reasons for the outbreak of the English Civil War does Russell refer to in Source 13?

Learning outcomes

Through your study in this section you should have developed an understanding of why the crisis of 1637 radicalised the period 1640 to 1642, and why a royalist party formed. You should also be able to explain the inter-relation between the reasons for the English Civil War.

 Examination-style questions

(a) Explain why Thomas Wentworth was an important figure in the years 1639 to 1641. *(12 marks)*

 Take note of the dates in the question. There should be some comment/example linked to these dates. Explaining why the individual was important should incorporate an explanation of their role/position, what they did in the specified period or why they were a focus for others in the specified period.

Wentworth can be considered in relation to the following:

- Briefly what he had done in Ireland to 1639 and the consequences in the period 1639–41.
- Why Charles brought him back to England.
- Why he was the focus of parliamentary attack.
- The political consequences of the attack on Wentworth.

(b) 'Developments in Scotland and Ireland, 1637–42, were responsible for the outbreak of civil war in England in 1642.' Explain whether you agree or disagree with this view.

(24 marks)

In answering such a question it is important that you structure your answer appropriately so that you:

■ address the specific wording of the question

■ cover the key content that will address the question and illustrate your argument

■ comment on the key content in relation to the question.

In revising for the exam and in planning a class essay, you may produce a detailed plan. This plan can be done in a linear fashion or you may find that it suits your learning style better to produce such plans and notes in other forms, e.g. mind maps. The main thing is that the plan and notes work for you.

It is important with such notes or plans that you also think about how you would comment on this material to specifically answer the question set.

You could add comments to the plan, indicating what kind of comments you might make in an essay.

You should also decide on your general argument, for example:

'Events in Scotland were key to the expression of discontent in England, it led to an English parliament as an institution to address the abuses of personal rule. But Charles' failure to accept settlement and radicalisation through the impact of Ireland and question of religion, led to the division of parliament and the formation of two sides necessary for a civil war.'

In explaining the outbreak of civil war in England, more focus, especially given the time limits in an exam, should be on the period that saw division in parliament –1641–2. In this period, crucial in causing division was the Militia Bill, which resulted from the Irish Rebellion. In explaining the division in parliament, some comment on constitutional royalism will strengthen answers.

Fig. 1 *Execution of Charles I*

On the surface, in 1642, England was very much as it had been when Charles I came to the throne in 1625. There was still a monarchy and the system of government was still a personal monarchy. Furthermore, the Church of England and the key institutions of the State remained in place. Charles had not deliberately aimed to become absolutist and had made no major radical reform of government. The key themes of 1625 to 1629 remained the key issues:

- The relationship between the crown and the political nation, represented in parliament.
- The finances of the crown.
- A national Protestant Church, within which there was a range of opinion and outside of which there were groups that sort a different form of religious settlement.
- The complicated relationship between the three kingdoms and their own internal divisions.

Yet, in 1642, England would have felt very different from how it had been when Charles I came to the throne. A country at peace with itself and other nations in 1625 had quickly become a country humilated when it had intervened in the contintental war in the 1620s, and in 1642 was on the verge of armed conflict among its own people. A civil war between crown and parliament was unknown in England but with that reality about to be unleashed the country also seemed on the point of sliding into the anarchy that had bedevilled Europe since the outbreak of the Thirty Years' War in 1618. In 1642, loyalty to the crown was being openly debated, the finances of the crown had collapsed, the authority of the Church of England could no longer be enforced and the kingdoms were at war with each other and in conflict internally. While Charles' rule to 1642 had not brought radical structural change to the political, religious, economic or social systems, the advent of civil war and the revolution that accompanied it, which he was a key factor in causing, was to bring radical change.

The Civil War can be said to of lasted until 1651 when the son of Charles I, Charles Stuart, and the Scottish troops he brought south with him were defeated by Oliver Cromwell at Worcester. It has been estimated that 3.7 per cent of England's population of 5 million died in the period 1642 to 1648. Scotland lost 6 per cent of its population, whereas Ireland suffered a staggering loss of as much as 40 per cent of its population. To set these figures in some kind of context, England lost a greater percentage of its population in the Civil War than it did in either of the World Wars of the 20th century. Furthermore, these 'British wars' and the collapse of royal authority unleashed more revolutionary forces that saw the emergence of radical groups like the Levellers, Diggers, Quakers and Muggletonians. In 1649, Charles I was publicly executed and there followed 11 years of rule without monarchy, a period dominated by Oliver Cromwell. Without civil war none of this would have been possible. It is also possible to see in the period after 1660, when personal monarchy and the Church of England was restored with the return of Charles I's son, Charles II, the continuing impact of the Civil War on the religious and political life of the three kingdoms. Superficially, the restoration of monarchy in 1660 saw a return to the system and institutions under which Charles I had ruled, but the period 1642 to 1660 had unleashed forces that were to bring greater change over the next century as 'Britain' moved from an early modern State to a modern State.

THE

Declaration and Standard

Of the *Levellers* of *England* ;
Delivered in a Speech to his Excellency the Lord Gen. *Fairfax*, on *Friday* last at White-Hall, by Mr. *Everard*, a late Member of the Army, and his Prophesie in reference thereunto ; shewing what will befall the Nobility and Gentry of this Nation, by their submitting to community ; With their invitation and promise unto the people, and their proceedings in *Windsor* Park, *Oatlands* Park, and severall other places ; also, the Examination and confession of the said Mr. *Everard* before his Excellency, the manner of his deportment with his Hat on, and his severall speeches and expressions, when he was commanded to put it off. Together with a List of the severall Regiments of Horse and Foot that have cast Lots to go for *Ireland.*

Imprinted at *London*, for *G. Laurenson*, *April* 23. 1649.

Fig. 2 *The declaration and standard of the levellers of England*

The review of the causes of the English Civil War in Chapter 10 suggests that one factor can be seen as most important in unleashing conflict on the three kingdoms: Charles I. In many ways, this is only to be expected for, in a system based on personal monarchy, the personality and policies of the monarch are always central. It does need, however, to be pointed out that Charles I was faced by some very large problems and his failure should be clearly set in the context of the enormous challenges of ruling 'Britain' in this period. The extent of these structural problems have led some historians, notably Conrad Russell, to question whether England was ungovernable in this period. These problems were particularly pronounced in relation to finance, religion and multiple kingdoms. These problems had a consequent impact on politics and the nature of the State.

With the accession of the King of Scotland, James VI, to the English throne in 1603 as James I, England and Scotland became tied together despite there being no formal union and the continued differences in law, government, culture and society between them. On top of this, was the relationship with the other Stuart kingdom, Ireland. What complicated the ruling of these multiple kingdoms the most was a fundamental aspect of 17th-century life – religion. Charles not only ruled multiple kingdoms, he ruled kingdoms that were divided from each other in terms of religion, and also internally divided in terms of religion.

Fig. 3 *James VI of Scotland and James I of England and Ireland*

On top of the complex issues of multiple kingdoms and religion, the historian Conrad Russell, developing the ideas of Gerald Aylmer, has also written of England being on the point of a 'functional breakdown' in the 1620s. Such was the limited nature of the English State in terms of a civil service but more particularly its finances, that it had become incapable of adequately dealing with some of the crucial areas of government, especially war. The pressure of war in the 1620s brought political tension to the surface as Charles sought to fund his foreign policy. Charles' financial policies of the 1630s could be construed at their most positive as an attempt to work a way through the financial problems of the English crown. This structural problem was a long-term problem that would hamper any king not just Charles and was never really addressed until after 1689 (see page 49).

These serious problems meant that whoever was monarch would find ruling 'Britain' difficult. James I certainly found the multiple kingdom context increasingly difficult and especially when set against the context of war in Europe after 1618. Yet, it appears that Charles' style of kingship and his policies exacerbated these structural tensions and led to what can be justifiably called the worst conflict in English history. 'Britain' may have become increasingly more complex to govern, but Charles was simply not suited to the role of kingship in such circumstances.

Whilst there were clearly longer-term issues and complex political, religious and financial questions that contributed to the shape of the years 1625 to 1642, and specifically to the outbreak of conflict in 1642 and then the shape of the period 1642 to 1660, it is of note that almost the only thing historians when writing of these years can agree on is the weakness of Charles I as a monarch. Not only did Charles I shape the period in a system of personal monarchy, it can also be said that his influence was a negative one overall. A range of historians from S. R. Gardiner in the 1890s to R. Cust in 2006 have judged Charles I, at best, as misguided, but certainly a political failure. Indeed, it is hard to claim that any monarch who starts a civil war and ends up being publicly executed could have been a political success. The 1997 assessment of the historian Young is appropriate. He argues that Charles 'lacked flexibility and overreacted when things did not go his way. Given a bad situation, he usually managed to make it worse'.

At the heart of Charles I's failure was the fact that he raised questions that were best left alone in the 17th century – in particular questions relating to the limits of the prerogative and whether people owed loyalty to the crown or God. The manner in which Charles set about imposing his prerogative and Laudianism was problematic. His style of rule invited the question as to whether he could be trusted to rule in a country that had no defined constitution and it was far too easy for some to believe that he aimed at absolutism and Catholicism, especially when he chose not to explain himself or acted in a high handed way. Charles' rule in the years 1625 to 1642 literally forced people into opposition. It is a measure of the nature of English political society that it took until 1642 for conflict to emerge. Even then, most wanted to avoid it. Equally, it is a measure of Charles' political failings that in such a society that valued consensus, no matter what the real religious and political divisions that existed were, civil war occured. It is unlikely that Charles was actually aiming to establish himself as absolute, but the collapse of his personal rule and his defeat in the civil wars that followed did much to ensure that absolutism could not be developed.

Glossary

A

Arminianism: a form of Protestantism that was a reaction to Puritanism and the desire for further reformation. Seen as the Protestants closest to Catholicism because of their emphasis on ceremony and outward forms of religion. They have also been referred to as anti-Calvinists or, more particularly in the period of the personal rule, as Laudians. The term 'Arminian' is derived from the Dutch theologian, Jacobus Arminius, who particularly attacked the Calvinist idea of predestination.

B

'British problem': term used by some historians to explain the problem of 'multiple kingdoms' in the early modern period.

C

Catholicism: branch of the Christian Church headed by the Pope. In the eyes of many English at the time, Catholicism was linked with absolutism and the threat of both was symbolised by the power of Spain.

conformity: the term for agreeing to the set practices and order of the Church of England imposed by the monarch as supreme governor and the bishops appointed by the monarch.

conspiracy theory: the belief that there is a plot, intrigue or a different explanation for an event or series of events. In this period, the most important was the idea that Charles' religious policies were actually designed to lead the Church of England back to Catholicism.

constitution: the rules by which a State is governed. At the time, there was no 'written constitution' and England was said to be governed by the 'ancient constitution', a system that had evolved over time. Part of this constitution included documents like the Magna Carta of 1215, but the working of the constitution depended upon trust between crown and parliament and the balance of the prerogative and privilege.

coup: an attempt to overthrow the set order or remove key leadership figures from power.

D

dowry: property or money brought by the bride to her husband, normally paid by the daughter's father. One of the reasons for the Spanish match early in this period was that the potential dowry paid by the Spanish would help to alleviate the financial problems of James I.

E

Episcopacy: church run by bishops. The Church of England had the monarch as Supreme Governor and then the Archbishop of Canterbury and the Archbishop of York. There were bishops underneath these to administer the discipline of the Church.

G

Great Chain of Being: contemporary phrase for the idea of the ordered society in the 17th century set in place by God and where everyone was tied to each other.

O

opposition: there was no organised opposition in the modern sense of the term and certainly no party or political parties. Political alignments were fluid rather than there being a consistently aligned opposition movement. The closest to this was the network of opponents of crown policy of which Pym became a prominent figure with the calling of parliament in 1640. In the long parliament, what made this network of opposition most cohesive was their shared religious agenda, which can be generalised as Puritan.

P

personal monarchy: the power of the crown in this period was theoretically absolute and this was supported by the concept of the Divine Right of Kings. In such a framework the monarch was government and expected to actively rule. Therefore, their personality and aims shaped policy and, thus, it was a system of personal monarchy.

Protestantism: churches separated from Catholicism by the Reformation. The Protestant Church of England had become established under Henry VIII and Elizabeth I.

Puritanism: a more radical form of Protestant who saw themselves as the 'godly' and sometimes referred to as 'the hotter sort of Protestant'. They sought a further reformation of the English Church to remove the vestiges of Catholicism that remained from the Reformation.

R

radicalism: those advocating far-reaching reform or appearing to subvert the prerogative of the monarch in this period were seen as radical. The perceived radicalism of Pym made him seem more threatening to moderates than Charles I, which led to a reaction that can be labelled 'constitutional royalism'.

S

sheriff: appointed by the monarch for each country. Collected revenues and were in charge of preserving order. Organised parliamentary elections but could not stand as an MP.

T

tyranny: unconstitutional rule or term that might be applied to absolutism. An absolute ruler would be seen as a tyrant.

V

vestments: elaborate robes that ministers of the Church of England were supposed to wear when conducting services.

Bibliography

Students

Durston, C. (1998) *Charles I*, Routledge.

Quintrell, B. (1993) *Charles I 1625–1640*, Longman.

The Stuart period

Anderson, A. (1999) *Stuart Britain 1603–1714*, Hodder.

Brice, K. (1994) *The Early Stuarts, 1603–1640*, Hodder.

Coward, B. (1997) *Stuart England, 1603–1714*, Longman.

Scarboro, D. (2005) *England 1625–1660*, Hodder.

Seel, G. E. and Smith, D. L. (2001) *The Early Stuart Kings, 1603–1642*, Routledge.

Sharp, D. (2000) *The Coming of the Civil War, 1603–49*, Heinemann Educational.

Wilkinson, R. (1999) *Years of Turmoil. Britain 1603–1714*, Hodder.

Teachers and extension

Cope, E. (1987) *Politics Without Parliaments 1629–1640*, Allen & Unwin.

Hughes, A. (1998) *The Causes of the English Civil War*, Macmillan.

Reeve, L. J. (1989) *Charles I and the Road to the Personal Rule*, Cambridge University Press.

Sharpe, K. (1992) *The Personal Rule of Charles I*, Yale.

Young, M. (1997) *Charles I*, Macmillan.

The Stuart period

Hirst, D. (1999) *England in Conflict 1603–1660*, Arnold.

Smith, D. L. (1998) *A History of the Modern British Isles 1603–1707*, Blackwell.

Acknowledgements

The author and publisher would like to thank the following for permission to reproduce material:

Source texts:

p7 Gaunt, P., *The British Civil Wars, 1637–1651*, Routledge, 1997; p7 Woolrych, A., *Britain in Revolution*, Oxford University Press, 2002; p11 Morrill, J., *Stuart Britain. A Very Short Introduction*, Oxford University Press, 2000; p11 Gaunt, P., *The British Civil Wars, 1637–51*, Routledge, 1997; p13 Quintrell, B., 'Report of the Tuscan Ambassador, 1625' in *Charles I 1625–1640*, Longman, 1993; p13 Cust, R., *Charles I*, Longman, 2005; p15 From Quintrell, B., *Charles I 1625–1640*, Longman, 1993; p16 (both) From Scarboro, D., *England 1625–1660*, Hodder, 2005; p19 Anon. Taken from Seel, G. E. and Smith, D. L., *The Early Stuart Kings, 1603–1642*, Routledge, 2001; p20 Sibthorpe's sermon, 'Apostolike Obedience', 1627; p28 From Daniels, C. W. and Morrill, J. (eds.), *Charles I*, Cambridge University Press, 1988; p29 Coward, B., *The Stuart Age*, Longman, 1994; p29 Morrill, J., *Stuart Britain. A Very Short Introduction*, Oxford University Press, 2000; p30 Russell, C., *Parliaments and English Politics 1621–9*, Oxford University Press, 1979; p31 Cust, R., *The Forced Loan and English Politics 1626–8*, Longman, 1987; p32 Brice, K., *The Early Stuarts, 1603–1640*, Hodder, 1994; p32 Smith, D. L., *A History of the Modern British Isles, 1603–1707*, Blackwell, 1998; p32 Quintrell, B., *Charles I 1625–1640*, Longman, 1993; p35 Atherton, I. and Sanders, J. (eds.), *The 1630s. Interdisciplinary essays on culture and politics in the Caroline era*, Manchester University Press, 2006; p36 Smith, D. L., *A History of the Modern British Isles, 1603–1707*, Blackwell, 1998; p37 Merritt, J. F. (ed.), *The Political World of Thomas Wentworth, Earl of Strafford, 1621–1641*, Cambridge University Press, 1996; p40 Young, M., *Charles I*, Macmillan, 1997; p40 Sharpe, K., *The Personal Rule of Charles I*, Yale, 1992; p41 Adapted from the Venetian Ambassador's report to the Doge and Senate of Venice, 25 April 1625. Taken from Daniels, C. W. and Morrill, J. (eds.), *Charles I*, Cambridge University Press, 1998; p41 Strong, R., *Art and Power*, Boydell, 1984; p42 Cust, R., *Charles I*, Longman, 2006; p43 Lake, P., 'Anti-Popery: the structure of a prejudice'. Taken from Cust, R. and Hughes, A. (eds.), *Conflict in Early Stuart England*, Longman, 1989; p48 Hirst, D., *England in Conflict, 1603–1660*, Arnold, 1999;

p49 Holstun, J., *Ehud's Dagger. Class Struggle in the English Revolution*, Verso, 2000; p50 Sharpe, K., *The Personal Rule of Charles I*, Yale, 1992; p50 Coward, B., *The Stuart Age*, Longman, 1994; p51 Schama, S., *A History of Britain, vol. 2, The British Wars 1603–1776*, BBC, 2003; p52 (both) Camden Society; p53 Canny, N., *From Reformation to Restoration: Ireland 1534–1660*, Helican, 1987; p53 Fincham, K. and Lake, P. 'The Ecclesiastical Policies of James I and Charles I'. Taken from Fincham, K. (ed.), *The Early Stuart Church, 1603–1642*, Macmillan, 1993; p54 Young, M., *Charles I*, Macmillan, 1997; p54 Cressy, D., *Travesties and Transgressions in Tudor and Stuart England*, Oxford University Press, 2000; p58 Seel, G. and Smith, D. L., *The Early Stuart Kings, 1603–1642*, Routledge, 2001; p58 Woolrych, A., *Britain in Revolution, 1625–1660*, Oxford University Press, 2002; p58 Impeachment Articles against Laud. Taken from Daniels, C. W. and Morrill, J. (eds.), *Charles I*, Cambridge University Press, 1998; p59 The Works of William Laud, vol.2, [a Relation of the Conference between William Laud and Mr Fisher the Jesuit, 1639]. Taken from Daniels, C. W. and Morrill, J. (eds.), *Charles I*, Cambridge University Press, 1998; p59 From Daniels, C. W. and Morrill, J. (eds.), *Charles I*, Cambridge University Press, 1998; p59 and p62 Coward, B., *The Stuart Age*, Longman, 1994; p63 Clarke, A., *A New History of Ireland. Early Modern Ireland, 1534–1691*, Clarendon Press, 1976; p65 Milton, A. in Merritt, J. F. (ed.), *The Political World of Thomas Wentworth, Earl of Strafford, 1621–1641*, Cambridge University Press, 1996; p66 Smith, D. L., *A History of the Modern British Isles, 1603–1707*, Blackwell, 1998; p67 Wheeler, J. S., *The Irish and British Wars 1637–1654*, Routledge, 2002; p69 Brown, K., *Kingdom or Province? Scotland and the Regal Union, 1603–1715*, Macmillan, 1992; p69 Wheeler, J. S., *The Irish and British Wars 1637–1654*, Routledge, 2002; p70 Cust, R., *Charles I*, Longman, 2006; p70 Young, M., *Charles I*, Macmillan, 1997; p70 Wilkinson, R., *Years of Turmoil. Britain 1603–1714*, Hodder, 1999; p73 From Daniels, C. W. and Morrill, J. (eds.), *Charles I*, Cambridge University Press, 1998; p73 Anderson, A., *Stuart Britain 1603–1714*, Hodder, 1999; p75 Smith, D. L., *A History of the Modern British Isles*, Blackwell, 1998; p76 From Quintrell, B., *1625–40*, Longman, 1993; p76 Hyde, E., *The History of the Rebellion*, reprinted 1958, Clarendon Press, 1888; p79 From Daniels, C. W. and Morrill, J. (eds.), *Charles I*, Cambridge University Press, 1998; p82 Woolrych, A., *Britain in Revolution*, Oxford

University Press, 2002; p82 Brice, K., *The Early Stuarts, 1603–1640*, Hodder, 1994; p88 Wilkinson, R., *Years of Turmoil. Britain 1603–1714*, Hodder, 1999; p88 Brice, K., *The Early Stuarts 1603–1640*, Hodder, 1994; p90 Smith, D. L., *A History of the Modern British Isles, 1603–1707*, Blackwell, 1998; p90 Cressy, D., *England on Edge. Crisis and Revolution 1640–1642*, Oxford University Press, 2006; p94 Fissel, M., *The Bishops' Wars. Charles I's campaigns against Scotland 1638–1640*, Cambridge University Press, 1994; p94 (No.s 6 and 7) From Daniels, C. W. and Morrill, J. (eds.), *Charles I*, Cambridge University Press, 1998; p94 Cust, R., *Charles I*, Longman, 2006; p95 From Quintrell, B., *Charles I 1625–40*, Longman, 1993; p95 and p97 Scott, D., *Politics and War in the three Stuart Kingdoms, 1637–49*, Palgrave Macmillan, 2004; p98 Fissel, M., *The Bishops' Wars. Charles I's campaigns against Scotland 1638–1640*, Cambridge University Press, 1994; p100 From Daniels, C. W. and Morrill, J. (eds.), *Charles I*, Cambridge University Press, 1998; p100 Wilkinson, R., *Years of Turmoil. Britain 1603–1714*, Hodder, 1999; p100 Anderson, A., *Stuart Britain 1603–1714*, Hodder, 1999; p104 From Scarboro, D., *England 1625–1660*, Hodder, 2005; p104 The Petition of Twelve Peers, August 1640; p105 Stone, L., *The Causes of the English Revolution*, Routledge, 1972; p106 Sommerville, J., *Ideology, property and the constitution*, Longman, 1989; p109 Kilburn and Milton, A., 'The public context of the trial and execution of Strafford'. Taken from Milton, A. in Merritt, J. F. (ed.), *The Political World of Thomas Wentworth, Earl of Strafford, 1621–1641*, Cambridge University Press, 1996; p109 John Pym's reply to Strafford's defence, 13 April 1641. AQA specimen paper, 2001; p110 The Earl of Strafford's last speech in his defence, 13 April 1641. AQA specimen paper, 2001; p112 and p113 (top) Hughes, A., *The Causes of the English Civil War*, Macmillan, 1998; p113 Ashton, R., *The City and the Court 1603–1643*, Cambridge University Press, 1979; p114 Brenner, R., *Merchants and Revolution. Commerical Change, Political Conflict, and London's Overseas Traders, 1550–1653*, Cambridge University Press, 1993; p114 (bottom) and p115 (top) From Petrie, C. A., *The Letters, Speeches and Proclamations of Charles I*, Cassell, 1968; p115 Cressy, D., *England on Edge. Crisis and Revolution 1640–1642*, Oxford University Press, 2006; p118 Morrill, J., *The Nature of the English Revolution*, Longman, 1993; p120 Adapted from Stone, L., *The Causes of the English Revolution*, Routledge, 1972; p120 Davies, J., *The Caroline Captivity of the Church: Charles I and the Remoulding of Anglicanism, 1625–1641*, Clarendon Press, 1992; p122 Seel, G. E. and Smith, D. L., *Crown and Parliaments*, Cambridge University Press, 2001; p124 From Scarboro, D., *England 1625–1660*, Hodder, 2005; p126 Brenner, R., *Merchants and Revolution. Commercial Change, Political Conflict, and London's Overseas Traders, 1550–1653*, Cambridge University Press, 1993; p128 From Petrie, C. A., *The Letters, Speeches and Proclamations of Charles I*, Cassell, 1968; p132 Bennett, M., *The English Civil War*, Longman, 1995; p133 Smith, D. L., *A History of the Modern British Isles, 1603–1707*, Blackwell, 1998; p133 Kishlansky, M., *A Monarchy Transformed. Britain 1603–1714*, Penguin, 1997; p134 Smith, D. L., *Constitutional Royalism and the Search for Settlement, c.1640–1649*, Cambridge University Press, 1994; p135 The Answer to the Nineteen Propositions; p135 Manning, B., *Aristocrats, Plebians and Revolution in England 1640–1660*, Pluto Press, 1996; p135 Cust, R., *Charles I*, Longman, 2006; p136 Hirst, D., *Authority and Conflict: England 1603–58*, Arnold, 1985; p137 Woolrych, A., *Britain in Revolution*, Oxford University Press, 2002; p137 Morrill, J., *The Nature of the English Revolution*, Longman, 1993; p138 Scott, D., *Politics and War in the Three Stuart Kingdoms, 1637–49*, Palgrave Macmillan, 2004; p139 Smith, D. L., *A History of the Modern British Isles, 1603–1707*, Blackwell, 1998; p141 Russell, C., *The British Problem and the English Civil War*, Hambledon Press, 1987

Photographs courtesy of:

Ann Ronan Picture Library pp12, 18, 25, 41, 45, 52, 53, 55, 57, 75, 79, 80, 81, 83, 89, 105, 109, 113, 117, 131, 137, 139, 144, 145; Edimedia Art Archive pp2, 15 (top and bottom), 22 (left), 22 (right), 34, 141; Getty Images piv; Manuscripts and Special Collections of the University of Nottingham p56; Mary Evans Picture Library pp28, 69, 110, 125; Topfoto pp10, 20, 42 (left), 42 (right), 87, 93 (top), 93 (bottom), 102, 108, 114, 127, 129, 138, 140; Topfoto/HIP pp63, 77, 86, 136; Topfoto/National Pictures p24; World History Archive pp4, 14, 23, 26, 37, 40, 46, 49, 51, 61, 112

Cover photograph: courtesy of Alamy/Andy Hallam

For further information concerning any pictures appearing in this book, please email samuel@uniquedimension.com.

Photo research by Unique Dimension Limited

Special thanks to Topfoto, Ann Asquith and Dora Swick

Index